BREAKTHROUGH
LEADERSHIP

*How Leaders Unlock the Potential
of the People They Lead*

Terry Lee

Order this book online at www.trafford.com
or email orders@trafford.com

Most Trafford titles are also available at major online book retailers.

Print information available on the last page.

ISBN 978-1-4907-9627-7 (sc)
ISBN: 978-1-4907-9630-7 (e)

Trafford rev.   07/31/2019

www.trafford.com
North America & international
toll-free: 1 888 232 4444 (USA & Canada)
fax: 812 355 4082

CONTENTS

Foreword

In December, 2001, Harvard Business Review devoted a special issue to the challenge of Breakthrough Leadership. It was this issue that inspired me at the time to better integrate my insights from psychology with my practice in leadership development so as to create more relevant, challenging and impactful programs to support managers in their development.

For me the challenge was as it always has been in my professional life.

1. understanding how leaders unlock the potential of the people that they lead
2. finding what they do to remove the barriers to that development.
3. helping to build cultures that grow the leadership potential in all of their people not just the few.

Breakthrough leadership was described as "breaking through old habits of thinking to uncover fresh solutions to perennial problems. It also means breaking through interpersonal barriers that we all erect against genuine human contact. It's leadership that breaks through the cynicism that many people feel about their job and helps them find meaning and purpose in what they do. And it breaks through the limits imposed by our doubts and fears to achieve more than we believed possible".

This book now is the culmination of nearly twenty years work in breakthrough leadership and began in the 1990's when I was head of the leadership group at Mt Eliza Business School in Melbourne. It subsequently became my passion understanding the distinctive people challenges in the companies that I have had the pleasure to work with since I set up my own consulting group, Leadership Psychology Australia, in 2001.

My interest, which was stimulated by my early training as a psychologist, was brought into sharp focus by the rapid changes taking place in leadership understanding and expectation as organisations sought ways to respond to global change. What started off as culture change programs in most organisations quickly became transformational change programs and the focus shifted from understanding the impact of values on employees to understanding the impact of their mindsets. Being a psychologist and having worked in clinical, counselling and developmental settings prior to work in executive development, I was looking at leadership from a psychological perspective and trying to help managers and executives to develop insight and expertise into the process of mindset change and personal growth.

Breakthrough leadership is the process by which leaders inspire their followers to grow, to perform and to develop their potential. They do this by understanding and helping to remove the impediments to that development. We know that many of the limitations that people place on themselves and their potential are related to their own self-limiting thinking. What we have found is that breakthrough leaders create a relationship and the support that gives followers the confidence to challenge the status quo and ultimately to challenge themselves and their development.

Breakthrough leaders build the self-confidence of their followers, they develop their capability, they unleash their courage to challenge and they deepen their conviction and belief in what they do. They use the power of purpose to bring deeper meaning to their work and to help people overcome self-doubt and to stimulate personal growth which might have stalled. This is not a quick fix and there is no absolute breakthrough, it is the on-going breakthroughs that we all make in our lives as we move through different stages and transitions. Throughout life we all need the support of teachers, parents and friends to grow and to thrive and it continues in our professional lives and is facilitated, and accelerated, with the understanding and support of thoughtful and caring leaders.

Kahlil Gibran when talking about change in his book "The Prophet" writes that "your pain is the breaking of the shell which encloses your understanding". This is an apt metaphor for the difficulty involved in mindset change. Change is not a painless process. It involves letting go of old ways of thinking before new ways of thinking can be embraced. Sometimes the old ways of thinking are reinforced by a lack of confidence, or a lack of self-belief in one's ability to meet the challenge of change. Sometimes they are reinforced by fear of uncertainty or of the unknown and sometimes they are "rusted on" by habit or by being in a "comfort zone".

Organisations globally have embraced performance cultures in their search for growth but also in response to rising expectations from a multitude of stakeholders. Managers have been trained in the skills of performance leadership and through processes such as performance management and performance appraisal there is broad acceptance that coaching is a key part of a manager's repertoire. Through this productivity has improved as people and teams have become more effective at hitting targets and also more efficient by doing so with less people, cost and in less time.

The next significant step in productivity and growth has been unlocking the potential of the people in those teams. Managers who have become very good at giving orders, will now have to become good at tapping talent. The "hidden value" that lies within organizations is the unrealized potential of the people within. Hiring good people and then making them even better is a distinct competitive advantage for excellent companies – some would suggest that it is the ultimate competitive advantage. Breakthrough leadership is a leadership style which is directed towards this challenge. Once managers have mastered the leadership of performance, the next step is the leadership of potential.

This book is an introduction to the concept of breakthrough leadership. It is a new frontier in leadership because it is concerned, not only with human behavior, but also with human psychology. It extends the role of leaders from a focus on the motivation and performance of the people they lead, to a concern for their mindset and development. The book provides some background to the trends in leadership and in particular to the emergence of transformational and inspirational leadership, it then outlines the research upon which the concept is based, explores the attributes of breakthrough leaders and finally outlines a framework for the development of breakthrough leadership capability.

Chapter One: Trends in Leadership

This chapter reviews the history of management and leadership from the Industrial Revolution. It explores how the theory and practice of leadership has evolved from a hierarchical model, through scientific management on to the humanistic model and then to the leader's role in inspiring the human spirit. These models all had a focus on behaviour and were in their own way significant milestones in our continuing understanding of the drivers of performance.

Chapter Two: Management and Leadership

This chapter highlights the shift in thinking that occurred as management and leadership began to be defined as discrete concepts. It describes the different roles played by managers and leaders and looks at how the emphasis on leadership eventually led to an appreciation of the leader's potential to transform people and culture.

Chapter Three: The Emergence of Transformational Leadership

This chapter discusses the theory of transformational leadership and distinguishes it from transactional approaches. The concept of the leader as first and foremost a servant of the people is introduced and there is a discussion about whether the real focus of transformational leadership is based upon the personality of the leader, the emotional connection with the follower or some other variable which essentially produces the inspiration to change. Breakthrough leadership is positioned under the umbrella of transformational leadership.

Chapter Four: What Transformational Leaders Really Do?

This chapter looks at what it is that leaders actually do. It describes the difference between leadership and management and then differentiates between good leadership and transformational leadership. It highlights the work of John Kotter and the research of Jim Kouzes and Barry Posner into personal best leadership. It concludes that to understand what makes leaders transformational it is necessary to identify not only what such leaders do, but also to understand the psychological impact of this on the mindset of the followers.

Chapter Five: Breakthrough Leadership

This chapter outlines our research into the nature of breakthrough leadership and specifically into discovering what it is that breakthrough leaders do. Breakthrough leaders are defined as leaders who help people to achieve their potential by breaking through old ways of thinking which are by their very nature self-limiting.

The research involved over 800 hundred managers who were asked to recall specific leaders who had inspired them to achieve more of their potential and in so doing had helped them to progress their careers to a higher level. The research identified six behaviours that were at the heart of the breakthrough experience. The impacts upon followers were identified and explained.

Chapter Six: The Practices of Breakthrough Leaders

This chapter discusses in more depth the six fundamental behaviours that define breakthrough leadership and describes their nature, application and impact. Each is discussed with the implications for leadership practice described.

Chapter Seven: The Attributes of Breakthrough Leaders

This chapter explores the personal characteristics of breakthrough leaders. It identifies eight core capabilities that energise and inspire the followers. Each characteristic is discussed in detail.

Chapter Eight: The Breakthrough Process

This chapter analyses the breakthrough process itself. It relates this process to the work of Edward De Bono and lateral thinking, Howard Gardner and frameworks for thinking and Martin Seligman and positive psychology. It outlines a model which explains the process, then relates the six behaviours to the stages in the model.

Chapter Nine: The Nature of Inspiration

Inspiration is the fuel which ignites the human spirit and powers the breakthrough process. It provides the energy required to break through the impediments to change and also the energy to sustain change over time. Bringing energy and inspiration to the workplace is an important element in creating the conditions for change. Leaders inspire through the relationships that they establish with the people they lead. The example of Bunnings Warehouse, a great Australian success story, is used to describe in a very practical way the development of breakthrough leaders or what they term high involvement leaders.

Chapter Ten: Redefining Success

This chapter outlines how the factors which drive organisational success have changed from the control driven structures of the past, to the people centred processes of the future. It describes how achieving greater discretionary effort has become the basis for sustainable competitive advantage. It concludes that those who excel will be those that secure the greatest discretionary effort by the greatest number, for the greatest time.

Chapter Eleven: Developing Breakthrough Leaders

The ability to develop breakthrough leaders is a strategic necessity in a rapidly changing world and the capacity to deploy them at all levels will be a significant driver of growth. It is well accepted that leadership bench strength is a driver of sustainable success, but it is less well understood how breakthrough leaders bring out the potential in the people they lead. Seven steps are outlined that can be employed to develop breakthrough leaders. It also describes a process whereby leaders can monitor their own development and provides two checklists that can be used to guide this development.

Conclusion: Making the Shift to More Effective Leadership

This chapter makes the final case for change in leadership style and practice. It discusses the mindset shift required and identifies some of the levers that will drive that change. It argues that this shift is not easy, but is inevitable, driven by the pursuit of higher performance in a rapidly changing world and the rising expectations of employees, customers, investors and communities.

Acknowledgments

My interest in this type of leadership and my understanding of the breakthrough process itself has been deepened by working in a very practical and applied way with excellent companies around the world and inspiring leaders throughout Asia, Europe, U.S, and Australia. My school of life has been primarily with, Honda, Fuji Xerox, Cisco Systems, CSL, Fosters, A.N.Z. Bank, Wesfarmers, Tabcorp, Clayton Utz lawyers, PwC and Centre for Creative leadership.

I have great confidence in the capacity of organisations to develop breakthrough leaders because I have seen so many of them in action. There are many unsung heroes around the world doing great work transforming workplaces and inspiring people to develop their full potential. I would like to acknowledge the friendship and contribution to my learning made by the many talented and passionate people I have had the pleasure to work with, and learn from, around the globe

Finally, my gratitude goes to Barbara who is my wife, partner, office manager and chief feedback consultant, for her never-ending support, her tireless work and her constant encouragement. She is truly the spark that ignites my human spirit.

Terry Lee
Sandringham, Australia.
February 2011, Revised April 2019
www.leadership.com.au

Introduction

The beginnings of breakthrough leadership

Globally today we face a significant leadership and management challenge. In many ways it is a challenge unlike that which has been faced before, and one which will determine the future of work and the nature of organisations in the future. It is less a challenge of behaviour and more a challenge of insight and thinking. It is a paradigm shift in the very concept of what it means to be a manager and to manage and lead others.

All organisations, whether they are in a competitive environment or not, whether they are government services or not-for-profits are facing the same reality and that is that the criteria by which their success is judged are shifting. Whereas once success was based around tangible resources or access to finance, today it is seen to be vested in the most intangible of all resources and that is the imagination and potential of people. It is not just who you have that is the key, but your ability to be able to extract more value from those people.

Sustainable success rests not simply with the people employed and the talent they display, but rather more the greater value they can contribute as their potential is developed and released. Growth will not come simply by putting more people on the payroll, nor from making those on the payroll more focussed or more contented. The stimulus for growth will come through developing the talent of each and every individual. Getting more from people, not getting more people, is the new formula.

For managers this requires a new understanding of what it means to lead people. Leadership has now become an essential part of the effective manager's repertoire. Managers need to understand what motivates and develops people, but just as importantly they need to appreciate what impedes human growth and development. Getting the best out of people requires a keen insight into human psychology and a broader perspective on the role and contribution of the human resources in any organisation.

Managers can no longer get by just on getting the job done. Ensuring task completion is no longer sufficient. Even driving performance is not enough and may even be counter productive if the results are achieved in a way which disengages people and undermines their long term commitment. Management will no longer be in demand if it is delivered in a way which excludes leadership. The growing demand will be for managers who know how to lead and for leaders who know how to manage. Management will be essential for being in the game and delivering what customers want. Leadership will determine those that win the game and sustain their success. Management is a role, but leadership will be the critical capability. Having strong leaders at all levels will not be optional, it will be regarded as the blueprint for survival.

The Hidden Value Inside Organisations

It is well accepted that hiring talented people and keeping talented people are two separate issues. Companies can hire the best people, but poor leadership and a mediocre culture can quickly dissipate any advantage gained. Landmark research from Stanford University by Charles O'Reilly and Jeffrey Pfeffer has shown that the best companies sustain their competitive advantage by a set of disciplined processes which bring out the best in the people employed. Growth and long-term success come from unlocking this hidden value. The real opportunity for companies lies in releasing what for so many remains as hidden potential.

To do this requires a new type of leader, one who can break through the barriers that prevent people from achieving their potential.

The companies studied by O'Reilly and Pfeffer, not only had a strategic edge which gave them a clear point of differentiation, but they also had an ability to create a strong enduring culture which not only supported the strategy and brought it to life, but also brought out the best in the people employed to deliver it. South-West airlines was one of the first to promote that they hired on attitude to get the right culture, and then taught the skills to get the right capabilities. Their success was not just determined by their business model, it was more driven by their preparedness to put in place practices and policies which developed and engaged their people. They regarded their people and their talent and commitment as their distinctive asset and they had leaders at all levels who not only nurtured people but also were prepared to be role models for them as well.

Traditional managers were good at controlling people, providing direction and supervising work, but had very little incentive to be concerned with people development. They were hired to manage and allocate resources and to reduce the complexity of the workplace in order to achieve clearly defined outcomes. They were expected to deal with tangible outcomes and not something as intangible as human potential. The tools that they had at their disposal were designed to measure, monitor and manage the systems and procedures that produced those results. Those used to measure performance were applicable to measuring what is (ie. current reality), but had very little to offer if measuring what might be (ie. future potential).

Autocratic managers and those who used a "command and control" style were more likely to have an obsessive attachment to direction, with more of their energy devoted to restricting variation and suppressing initiative than in liberating energy and giving people the freedom to decide. These were transactional managers, more attuned to creating dependency than building independence, better at producing compliance than initiative and leadership.

A more competitive global environment has lifted the performance stakes. A globalising world with global companies, global markets and global competition has resulted in hyper competition. What was once regarded as good has become, in many ways, average, and only the exceptional can be guaranteed long term success. The dramatic rate of change has also brought speed into the equation. This is not an environment where incremental change is a sufficient. A world of rapid change means that continuous improvement will not keep up with the pace required. It is not surprising that business leaders are looking for large scale change and change that is truly transformational. This is less about changing structure, more about changing the people within.

Transformational Change

The first steps in this drive for transformation were directed towards pushing decision-making and accountability down to the frontline. Taking the power in these areas from the bosses and giving it to the workers concerned was a central feature in the empowerment process. This radical change in the balance of power was not something that could be achieved by transactional management models. This has required a new type of leadership.

The idea of the transformational leader was someone who would not only change the behaviour of employees, but would in some way change their engagement and how they thought about the workplace. The transformational leader was primarily concerned with changing mindsets – changing thinking, attitudes and beliefs – beliefs that often workers had about themselves and their potential contribution. It meant that managers could no longer only be concerned simply with behaviours exhibited, but had to understand psychology and the drivers of peak performance.

This interest in transformation is in large measure a reflection of the competitive pressures that companies face due to the unprecedented increase in the pace of change. When there is low turbulence and low expectations from stakeholders about greatly improved performance then a "more of the same" strategy can be effective and in this case a directive management style is sufficient. This approach will not produce improvement but it will drive the consistency required in a business as usual strategy.

When the rate of change begins to gradually increase, and there is a need for some incremental adjustment to maintain competitiveness, then continuous improvement as an approach will keep pace. Typically, this produces a concerted effort from within to build a performance culture and this in turn necessitates a leadership style that is based upon coaching or capability development.

Rapid change and a high degree of turbulence produced by extreme competitive pressures requires highly adaptive cultures and the need to gain more from a workforce than even a performance culture is capable of producing. To succeed companies certainly need to tap the synergy that comes from better teamwork and more efficient and effective processes, but they also need to unlock the potential that lies within each individual within the team. It is no longer a matter of more people, nor of simply improved performance, but critically a matter of tapping into the potential that exist within each person. This is the essence of the transformational challenge.

Transformational Leadership

Transformational leadership was first differentiated from transactional leadership by James McGregor Burns in 1978 in his book "Leadership". Transactional leadership was described fundamentally as a management approach to leadership whereby the boss and the employee were joined together by a mutual benefit. The mutual benefit was exhibited every time that the employee worked and satisfied the boss's needs and received a benefit (eg. reward, recognition, appreciation) in return. Transformational leadership on the other hand was an approach whereby a relationship of trust was established between boss and employee and this relationship had an impact on the employee which produced greater commitment, greater enthusiasm, greater performance and better results from the individual. Transformational leadership was presented as a higher order leadership style and one which was built upon the foundations of transactional leadership.

Whilst charismatic or "great man" or "heroic" leadership concepts have been written about for centuries, transformational leadership came into prominence by the business need for large scale change and it led to a fundamental shift in thinking about the best way to organise and develop people. It also reflects the influence of humanistic psychology upon leadership thinking over the past fifty years and especially the early work of psychologists such as Abraham Maslow and Frederick Hertzberg and the more recent contributions of psychologists such as Howard Gardner and Daniel Goleman.

Early approaches to transformational leadership were most closely associated with charismatic leadership. These leaders were seen to transform by the force of their personal charisma. Many of the most famous, such as Jack Welch or Richard Branson, became celebrities in their own right, sought after internationally for their opinions and thoughts. They were iconic leaders who, it was believed, by force of their personal drive, could inspire their followers to emulate their feats.

The continued high expectations placed upon leaders today has sustained keen interest in what it is that they do which has such a dramatic impact on the performance of their people. Inspiration, or being inspired, is regarded as the driving force of the transformational process and identifying with a "hero" leader is believed by many to be a prime lever for stimulating change at the personal level. There is a wide spread fascination with the concept of charisma, whether or not it is in public life, in politics or in the business world. A great deal of attention is focused on understanding the qualities which define charisma and the processes by which these qualities are brought into play.

More recently, the idea of charisma as a basis for transformation has been challenged. The central argument against the role played by charisma in the transformational process is that whilst the personality of a leader can have a powerful effect, its impact is often short lived as it does little to sustain the actual process. Personal experience and a great deal of anecdotal evidence teach us that the impact of the leader has usually waned by the time that the inspiration of the employee hits the realities of everyday life. The half time motivational address of the passionate football coach might provide an instant hit of motivation, but this usually fades quickly once play resumes and the realities of the game take hold.

Breakthrough Leadership

A more recent trend has been to explore less the example of the leader and more the process of transformation in the mind of the employee. Is it something external to the person or something within the person which inspires, and does so in a way which sustains transformation? This approach, referred to as breakthrough leadership, takes the view that the prime process involved in transformation is breaking through patterns of thinking which can be described as self-limiting or self-defeating. The purpose is to inspire a person to challenge their own mindset which may ultimately be the major inhibiting factor to their own development.

Bringing out the best in people is a simple concept, but a complex process. It requires an understanding of what drives human behaviour and what motivates individuals. Each individual's motivation is uniquely theirs. It is a complex structure of values and needs, aspirations and past experience. Each of these elements is brought together and blended into what is called a mindset. It is this mindset which determines motivation and which frames aspiration. The mindset can be self-enhancing or it can be self-limiting or it may vary according to personal judgements and perceptions at any particular time.

What is certain is that one's mindset can be an asset or it can be an impediment to one's growth and development. It can open doors and it can close doors. What it means is that leaders who wish to develop their people, and who determine their own success through the outcomes achieved by their people, must understand human psychology and must appreciate the role that they can play in developing human potential.

Not all failure to achieve potential can be attributed to a self-defeating mindset. Some is due to a lack of opportunity, some to competing priorities and some to being in the wrong job at the wrong time. Many people plateau in their achievement. They reach a stage of development and then they seem to stop. This is commonly referred to as being in a comfort zone or explained by that old adage, that you "can't teach an old dog new tricks".

However, it is clear that effective leadership can inspire people to greater achievement and can play a significant role in the realisation of their potential. When underachievement is related to mindset, then leaders deploying the skills of breakthrough leadership will be the most effective. It is in this way that breakthrough leadership can be the stimulus for transformation, and breakthrough leaders at all levels can be significant agents for change.

It is clear that the transformational process is essentially driven by two types of leaders – charismatic and breakthrough – both using inspiration as the fuel for change. To overcome inertia and resistance to change, both use inspiration as the energizer for change. Charismatic leaders use their own personal example as the stimulus for inspiration, whereas breakthrough leaders use the relationship to build self-belief and confidence and to overcome "self-limiting" thinking which restricts their followers' growth.

Charisma has long been regarded as the driving force behind such transformation and the focus has been on charismatic leaders who, through the force and impact of their personalities, could inspire and motivate others to change. Whilst recognising that charisma can play an important role in motivation and developing aspiration, the breakthrough leader plays a critical role in sustaining and carrying this process through. Charismatic leaders can initiate the process through their own energy and passion, but this inspired feeling in most cases does not last without the support of a leader who is prepared to set aside time, over the long haul, to build confidence and capability.

Certainly. inspiration is the key which powers the change process. For most of us, breaking through habitual ways of thinking requires considerable energy to overcome the inertia that is a consequence of ingrained patterns of behaviour. It also requires a great deal of resilience to overcome the numerous setbacks which inevitably occur in any change process. But what it is that breakthrough leaders actually do has remained something of a mystery, even though recent research has begun to look into the nature of the interaction between the leader and follower.

What Breakthrough Leaders Do

For years I have been studying the power of inspiration in the workplace and seeking to identify what it is that breakthrough leaders do. Using hundreds of in-depth case studies of organisations and leaders, I have been able to delineate the behaviours that drive the breakthrough process and understand more clearly the nature of these leaders and the impact that they have on their followers. It is not a story of "hero" leaders and "larger than life" characters. It is really a story of ordinary leaders who, often in a low key way, make a huge difference to the lives of the people they lead. The real breakthrough leaders are the leaders and managers at all levels who every day bring out the best in the people they lead.

While inspiration can stem from the power of the vision, and how a person's work contributes towards that vision, breaking through old ways of thinking and behaving in the workplace more likely stems from the personal relationship with the leader each person reports to. This happens best when leaders are able to tap into the passion of each individual so as to understand what truly motivates them and then are able to provide the challenge, support and encouragement needed by each to reach his or her potential.

The real hidden value in organisations is not getting good people to come to work, nor even in getting them to perform effectively, although both are critical to success. The real hidden value lies in the potential, so far unrealised, of what lies largely dormant within the entire workforce. The strategic value that great leaders bring is their ability to recognise this potential, to bring it out and finally to deploy it in the best interests of the firm.

This is not simply about having great places to work as an end in itself. The real story is about sustainability and survival. It is because a great culture and being a great place to work enables a company to be better at executing its strategy than its competitors. It is not the strategy which brings competitive advantage, but the capacity to execute it that is the key. If employees will not bring the strategy to life in their daily interactions with customers then the strategy is little more than wishful thinking.

Certainly, cost pressures for companies means there is a need to get greater productivity from the people employed, but equally important is the need to get better ideas and more effective contribution from those same people. The competitive advantage of the future will increasingly be in the ideas that can be brought into play and quickly turned into innovation in processes, products and services. Transforming the way we work with people, and the way we develop people and engage people is the current and future leadership challenge.

Chapter 1

Trends in Leadership

From scientific management to humanistic psychology

The industrial revolution in the 19th century brought about a significant transition in the management of people and the structure of organisations. Moving from an Agrarian Economy to an Industrial Economy brought with it the need to manage large numbers of manual workers who were brought into cities and factories from farms and from the land. Management models were borrowed from the dominant large institutions of the times – the Military and the Church - and this institutionalized hierarchy and the pyramid structure as the new business model.

The managerial mindset of the times was built upon the central premise that people basically lacked motivation and initiative and would only work if directed. The underlying principle was that the workforce in general, could not be trusted to work without supervision. Regardless of whether this was due to lack of competence or some perceived defect of character, it meant that the key management preoccupation of the times was to control behaviour. This entrenched command and control management as the managerial paradigm of the industrial age.

Command and Control Management

Both command and control management and the hierarchical structure came to dominate work-life for over two centuries to the present day. Both produced certainty and "no surprises", but also locked in resistance to change and embedded it in the fabric of the organisations that were built. This has resulted in businesses centuries later that are still under-performing and resistant to change.

These organisations have had their day, even though in their time they were seen as effective. They were fit for purpose in an industrial world where labour was a commodity, where workers were interchangeable and where the machines and mechanical processes contained the real value. They introduced supervision as a key role for management and this enshrined control through supervision at successive layers up through the hierarchy to the top.

The rules and procedures, which flourished as bureaucracy grew, institutionalised this control and the manager's duty was to ensure that correct rules and procedures were followed regardless of circumstance. There was little room for initiative and all too often discretionary behaviour was considered to be a distraction from the task at hand. Management was concerned with securing required behaviour and, as a consequence, with implementing managerial processes and practices to ensure that compliance occurred. In the more enlightened bureaucracies, some contingent reinforcement was used where a variety of rewards and punishments, or carrots and sticks, were introduced to shape behaviour.

In essence people were paid for attendance, not for what they accomplished, and were rewarded irrespective of outcome. There was little incentive for performance and in many cases the work typically expanded to fill in the time made available for the task. Not surprisingly, these were not high performing organisations, in that they placed a low priority on personal achievement and on the development of human potential.

In a world of low-level competition, where the expectations of staff, customers and investors were modest, it is not surprising that the standards set were not high. This particularly suited companies that were monopolies or government controlled and that faced no competition. Managers could thrive without being stretched and could survive with what would be considered by today's standards, fairly mediocre performance. This was before the introduction of performance cultures and the processes designed to drive performance, such as key performance indicators, and performance management systems.

These approaches to the management of people began to change after World War 2. The changes, in part, were a consequence of the world becoming more globally competitive. There was also a change in management style as organisations began to adopt some of the leadership practices that returned soldiers had been taught during the war. The great investment in tertiary education made after the war in all western societies and the opening up of these institutions to a broader range of students accelerated these trends.

Scientific Management

The first big challenge to management thinking, however, was brought about by what was known as Scientific Management. It was considered by many to be a great breakthrough in thinking and was championed by Frederick Winslow Taylor as a way of improving the relationship between managers and workers by putting that relationship on a scientific basis. It was intended to promote growth and increase productivity.

Taylor wrote that "the great revolution that takes place in the mental attitude of the two parties under Scientific Management is that both sides take their eyes off the division of the surplus as the all important matter, and together turn their attention towards increasing the size of this surplus until this surplus becomes so large that it is unnecessary to quarrel over how it shall be divided."

Taylor believed that a mental revolution was required and one that recognised the sovereignty of science. He wanted to remove opinion, personal preference and all manner of subjective influence from the workings of management and to substitute this with objective science. He was advocating a "complete mental revolution" – what we now call a paradigm shift.

Taylorism became associated with time management processes and the introduction of the assembly line and in its day, it produced huge leaps in productivity and efficiency. It put the system ahead of the person and the process ahead of even performance because in the end, both were to be followed even if performance was to suffer. Taylor was able to identify many of the variables that led to greater efficiency but few that applied to the human spirit or to ways to improve intrinsic motivation or commitment.

Under Scientific Management, orders went one way and that was top down, never back up the other way, and this reinforced command and control management style by putting it on a scientific basis. Its intent had been to remove variations in managerial behaviour caused by differences in personality and to, in fact, make it more certain. Workers were to follow orders without question and to implement procedures even if they made no sense to the worker concerned. This created a strong dependence on the system and the boss and it created a workforce that was by design passive and compliant. The individual was not central to the picture, the process was, and workers were just another component within a complex industrial process which had to be managed.

Humanistic Psychology

Management theory began to change in the second half of the twentieth century when the philosophy of leadership was introduced to the science of management. Propelled by the boom in post war economies and the aspirations for a better world after the horrors of World War 2, and inspired by the humanistic psychology movement of the nineteen sixties, a new revolution took place that began to explore human potential. These theories promoted the view that humans were a growth oriented species and that development was an inevitable part of that growth process. They regarded learning as intrinsic to development and fulfilment of one's potential as being the ultimate goal of life.

A central figure was Abraham Maslow who described a hierarchy of needs as a way to explain motivation. He argued that human motivation was driven more by the satisfaction of personal needs than external factors. That in effect it was intrinsic motivation rather than extrinsic which was the more powerful. Maslow also argued that these needs were arranged, and in fact satisfied, in a hierarchy from lowest to highest; the lowest needs being for physiological satisfaction and these in turn lead all the way up to the satisfaction of needs for self-actualisation or the ultimate achievement of human potential.

At the same time Frederick Herzberg introduced his motivator-hygiene theory or two factor theory which differentiated between factors which produce job satisfaction (motivators) and factors which produce job dissatisfaction (hygiene factors). He suggested that motivators were associated with intrinsic aspects of the work such as achievement and recognition whereas hygiene factors were to do with the context of the work, for example company policy, job benefits and salary. He argued that people would not perform unless these hygiene factors were catered for, but cautioned that simply providing more would not produce greater motivation – this would come from the supply of motivating factors.

Another writer with a significant influence in humanistic psychology was Douglas McGregor. In "The Human Side of Enterprize", he launched a scathing attack on the command and control view of the world. He put forward a set of assumptions called Theory X and Theory Y which he explained were two contrasting views about the nature of man which produced significant variations in managerial behaviour.

He described the conventional managerial mindset as one built upon the assumption of the mediocrity of the masses. The central tenets of what he described as Theory X were:

- Most people have an inherent dislike of work and will avoid it if possible
- People need to be directed because they want to avoid responsibility and want security above all
- People need therefore to be coerced, controlled and directed

He described the opposite assumptions as Theory Y:

- Putting effort into work is as natural as play or rest
- People don't dislike work, it's more the jobs they are given
- Control and punishment are not the best motivators
- Commitment to work is related to need satisfaction
- Under favourable conditions, people welcome responsibility
- The capacity for innovation and initiative is widely, not narrowly, distributed in the population

Proctor and Gamble took on board many of McGregor's ideas with a culture change program which sought to shift their plants from acting on the basis of Theory X to acting on the basis of Theory Y. Over a decade from the mid-sixties, Proctor and Gamble achieved productivity jumps of around thirty percent in the plants they converted. This was tangible evidence that a new approach to management, one that was more participative and designed to enhance human potential, could produce superior results.

The Influence of Tom Peters

In 1982 an iconic business book, "In Search of Excellence: lessons from America's best run companies", was published by Tom Peters and Robert Waterman. At the time both were McKinsey consultants and they set out to identify the success ingredients of companies which were regarded as being outstanding performers. This book had a huge impact on thinking about corporate culture, leadership and performance and it was the forerunner in a series of books purporting to discover the success secrets of highly successful companies.

Its success formula was:

1. A bias for action
2. Closeness to the customer
3. Autonomy and entrepreneurship
4. Productivity through people
5. Hands on, value driven

6. Stick to the knitting
7. Simple form, lean staff
8. Simultaneous loose-tight properties

"In Search of Excellence" was in many ways a recipe book and its ingredients became celebrated in their own right and most were embraced enthusiastically by corporate leaders of the time. It placed people, both customers and workers, as central ingredients of success and relationships as the barometers of success. There was little reference to structure or to science, and most of the emphasis was on people and the factors that had an impact on people. There was little about management more about leadership.

This book was followed in 1985 by "A Passion for Excellence" published by Peters and Nancy Austin. This book paid much greater attention to leadership and the role of the leader which was, according to Peters, a deficiency of the previous book. They introduced the idea of M.B.W.A., "management by wandering around", and highlighted the importance of the relationship between the leader and follower and specifically the nature of the communication which took place.

They highlighted coaching and counselling as key leadership functions which when they were done properly were the most effective method for addressing problems in performance. In this book they put the leader at the centre of performance and stressed the critical importance of the relationship in this process. They maintained that "leaders must look in the mirror first, have trust and integrity, and bring the company's values to life."

To complete the trilogy in 1987, Peters released "Thriving on Chaos" where he made the case for a revolution in management as the only appropriate response to globalisation and the rapid rate of change. He made the case for managers to stop treating their workers with "contempt" if they are truly interested in building quality goods and services. He placed great store in the "stump speech" which he described as a brief talk (three to five minutes) which effective leaders delivered to bring the vision to life in the minds of their followers. He regarded this speech as a major vehicle for change and the prime way to inspire people to higher performance.

He described the leadership recipe for success as:

1. Be out and about
2. Demand empiricism
3. Listen
4. Learn to love failure
5. Proclaim the virtue of speedy action
6. Talk up the common denominators
7. Let the customers do the teaching
8. Make it fun
9. Promote those who deal with paradox

Peters moved beyond strategy and culture as drivers of performance to elevate the role of the leaders. For the first time we find expounded in popular management literature the process by which managers inspire their followers to higher performance and a clear outline of the characteristics that make them inspirational leaders. Over the course of these books Peters became more specific about behaviour and more detailed about the small things that leaders do which make such a great difference to performance and engagement.

Chapter 2

Management and Leadership

Making the distinction

Clearly one of the major developments in management theory has been the distinction made between leadership and management as constructs and as applied models. This resulted in, and enabled, a greater focus on people development as a management function. It also produced a concern for personal development and self-awareness as management development issues. It resulted in greatly increased expectations of managers by all stakeholder groups and greater scrutiny of their performance.

The change in definition did not drive these changes as they were more a reflection of changes that were in train in the workplace, but what it did was to open up the debate about the value managers add and the role they play. Leadership became something that managers at all levels must exhibit and something that all organisations must develop as a core capability if they wished to survive. Whether it was managers at the frontline or those in executive ranks, leadership became a central component of a manager's role

Peter Drucker, one of the foremost management thinkers of his generation, was amongst the first to formally propose a distinction between management and leadership. Known for his ability to bring clarity to what are often complex management debates, Drucker proposed simply that managers "do things right" whereas leaders "do the right thing".

What really ignited the debate though was the publication of an article in 1977 in the Harvard Business Review by Abraham Zaleznik, a Professor of Leadership at the Harvard Business School. This article at the time was quite provocative and outlined in some detail what he saw as the differences between leadership and management. In a retrospective commentary, Zaleznik reflected on the controversy caused by his article at the time:

When 'Managers and Leaders: are they different' first appeared in the Harvard Business Review practising managers and academics thought I had taken leave of my senses."

For Zaleznik the key distinction between management and leadership was:

"A managerial culture emphasizes rationality and control. Whether his or her energies are directed toward goals, resources, structures or people, a manager is a problem solver. Leaders work in the opposite direction. Where managers act to limit choices, leaders develop fresh approaches to long standing problems and open issues to new options. To be effective leaders must project their ideas onto images that excite people."

In 1989 Max De Pree proposed leadership as an art and compared the science of management with the art of leadership and reinforced Drucker's view that leadership is concerned primarily with effectiveness, rather than efficiency. "Leaders can delegate efficiency but they must deal personally with effectiveness", stated De Pree. Effectiveness for him meant helping others in reaching their potential and in becoming better leaders in their own right.

De Pree wrote that the challenge to leaders is in understanding that "effectiveness comes about through enabling others to reach their potential – both their personal potential and their corporate potential" and that the privilege of leadership is "having the opportunity to make a meaningful difference in the lives of those who permit leaders to lead."

He argued that "the goal of thinking hard about leadership is not to produce great or charismatic leaders. The signs of outstanding leadership appear primarily among the followers. Are the followers reaching their potential? Are they learning? Serving? Do they achieve the required results? Do they change with grace? Manage conflict?"

Understanding What Managers and Leaders Do

John Kotter, also from Harvard University reinforced the difference between the two concepts and this resulted in widespread public acceptance of the split.

Kotter's view was that:

"Leadership was different from management. It has nothing to do with having charisma or other exotic personality traits. Rather leadership and management are two distinctive and complementary systems of action. Each has its own function and characteristic activities. Both are necessary for success in an increasingly complex and volatile business environment.... The real challenge is to combine strong leadership and strong management and to use each to balance the other".

Kotter wrote that management is concerned with control and pushing people in the right direction whereas leadership is more concerned with motivating people by satisfying their basic human needs. From this perspective, for a manager control is something administered externally to the person, whilst for a leader control is something intrinsic to the person's nature and requires leaders to have a deep understanding of the motives and needs of their followers.

Kotter was one of the first to provide a framework which clearly differentiated the behaviour of leaders from those displayed by managers. He observed that what managers and leaders do are fundamentally different and that this difference becomes more critical in a rapidly changing global environment.

"Management is about coping with complexity. Its practices and procedures are largely a response to one of the most significant developments of the twentieth century: the emergence of large organisations. Without good management, complex organisations tend to become chaotic in ways that threaten their very existence. Good management brings a degree of order and consistency.

Leadership by contrast, is about coping with change. Part of the reason that it has become so important is that the business world has become more competitive and more volatile. Major change is becoming a way of life to survive and to compete effectively in this new environment. More change always demands more leadership."

He described management as:

- Planning and budgeting
- Organising and staffing
- Controlling and problem solving

In contrast, he described leadership as:

- Setting direction
- Aligning people
- Motivating people

Setting a direction is not simply about planning. Planning is a deductive process once decisions have been made and conclusions drawn, whereas direction setting is inductive and involves the quest for vision and strategy. It means that leaders need skills to stimulate debate, gather ideas, facilitate discussion and to formulate diverse views into a common perspective. They need to do this in the context of a vision that can be shared by all and can be used to create alignment across a complex, diverse organisation.

Aligning people is not simply concerned with the supply of people and the deployment of people. It is more concerned with getting the right people and putting them in the right positions where they can work most effectively together. Leaders need skills in understanding difference and bringing people with different values together, and skills in communication and in delegating and empowering people. Gaining greater engagement is a challenge, especially those that are globally dispersed. Where once close supervision ensured that people were aligned, increasingly it is the corporate culture which provides the cohesion.

As well as recognising that management and leadership are two separate things, a great deal of contemporary research is devoted to the impact of corporate culture upon performance and the prime role that is played by leaders in building and directing that culture. John Kotter was also a pioneer in this field and his research into corporate culture and performance surprised the business world when he identified the extent to which culture has an impact on performance, especially financial performance. His research, published in 1992, demonstrated that great corporate cultures produced superior results on almost all measures (revenue, profit etc.) when compared with companies which had poor cultures. It placed leadership, and most importantly the behaviour of the leaders, as central to producing a great corporate culture.

Leadership and Culture and Performance

This brought a new element into the performance equation, that of organisational culture, and it established the central importance of leadership in driving that culture. This led to a surge of interest in leadership, culture and performance and into ways to change corporate culture in order to boost business performance.

"Built to Last" published in 1994, was an important contributor to this debate. Written by Jim Collins and Jerry Porras from Stanford

University, it looked at the success secrets of long-term successful companies. It highlighted the role of leaders at all levels and the importance of aligning their behaviour with the values espoused in the culture. It also initiated a great deal of discussion about the power of vision to motivate people and about the importance of building the right culture. The right culture they defined as one that aligned with people's values and one which was consistent with the business strategy.

Jim Collins continued this theme in "From Good to Great", where he stressed that the shift from good to great was more about getting the people side of the business right, rather than coming up with a world beating strategy. He moved the debate onto the character of the leader and he proposed the great leader as a proponent of "level five leadership". This he said was a leadership style that combines humility with a fierce determination to succeed. His research pointed to Level Five Leadership as the style required to achieve greatness.

The significant leaps that we have seen in productivity in global companies over the past two hundred years has required fundamental rethinking about the ways we motivate, mobilise and engage diverse workforces. In its day thinking was dominated by Scientific Management and then the Humanistic Psychology Movement, and more recently the impact of leadership and corporate culture.

At the same time an emphasis has been placed on continuous improvement and incremental changes. This has produced important, but marginal, increases in performance. Typical of these approaches have been transactional management techniques, which favour bottom line, cost driven, efficiency measures. These certainly make companies more competitive by removing duplication and waste and reducing costs, but alone they fail to deliver the large leaps in performance that top line, effectiveness driven measures are designed to produce.

The need in an increasingly competitive world for even greater leaps in performance has drawn attention to what is called transformational leadership. In this approach the focus is on the power of vision, and the need to build cultures which tap greater human engagement, commitment and accountability. This is all leadership – the ability to inspire people to go beyond what they think is possible in the pursuit of a worthwhile and meaningful vision.

Inspirational Leadership

But what is it that motivates people toward exceptional performance? Two dominant fields of thought emerged. One that people are inspired by the example of charismatic leaders and heroic figures who tap into a vein of repressed aspiration and who through their own behaviour provide an example of what is possible.

This approach puts forward the view that the charismatic leaders inspire through their own personal achievement. Through their life they provide a model of what is possible and that their followers identify with this and seek to emulate them. The affinity the followers have with the leaders means that they see aspects of their own characteristics which are similar to those possessed by the leader and the admiration drives them to develop these shared characteristics.

Political figures such as Martin Luther King or Nelson Mandela or Barak Obama would be examples of the charismatic style. In a business context, leaders such as Richard Branson, Steve Jobs or Elon Musk, who would be regarded by many as charismatic leaders, were able to become celebrities in their own right.

The other approach suggests that the impact of charismatic leaders is at best transitory and that what inspires people in a more lasting way is the nature of the relationship with the leader. This position takes the view that people are inspired when they have a relationship with a leader who genuinely believes in them and their potential and who works closely with them to remove impediments to the development of that potential. This requires leaders to be adept at mindset change and especially the challenging of overcoming self-limiting or self-defeating thinking.

This approach is based on the belief that charismatic leaders can certainly motivate, but do little to actually change the personal psychology of followers. Their motivation, whilst powerful at the time, soon runs out of steam when faced with the reality of daily life. For people to fundamentally change, they need the confidence and the courage to challenge their own doubts and fears and they then need support and encouragement to enable them to see it through.

It is not the desire to change which is the problem, it is more the resilience to see it through. For this people need coaches, mentors and leaders who accept that a major part of their role is the development of others. Kenneth and Miriam Clarke from the Center for Creative Leadership described the difference this way:

"Although transformational leadership as a concept places less emphasis on the personal qualities of the leader and more on a set of specific behaviours of the leader and followers, the descriptions of the behaviours are quite similar to those of charismatic leaders. However, transformational leaders inspire greater involvement in work and assure more self fulfilment by increasing the intellectual and emotional involvement of followers. A vision is articulated; the reasons for decisions are explained; goals are set and sold to the group so that they are accepted; the transformational leader works to engender trust and respect."

Some writers have suggested that these two fields of thought might reflect differences in national character, especially as it applies to management, between a U.S. approach and a European approach. The U.S. approach, where heroes are lauded and the individual is supreme and where the senior leader is often a celebrity figure is contrasted with a European perspective which they describe as having more of a focus on collaboration and the team.

Despite differences in perspective, interest in charisma has long held a place in the global imagination. Some would say that there is something in the human psyche which expresses a need for a father, or mother figure. That there is a deep desire embedded in humans for someone to take responsibility, to take charge and to solve problems. This view is that people have a need for heroes, and that this could in part explain the celebrity status given to many contemporary business leaders.

However, the question remains: do charismatic leaders actually produce real and lasting change in their followers or does the motivation they produce fade without leaders closer to the scene who do the personal work of inspiration with a more immediate practical focus?

Chapter 3

The Emergence of
Transformational Leadership

What transformation means

The emerging challenge for leaders today is the challenge of transformation. The challenge to fundamentally change the nature of organisations and the relationship they have with their people and through this to unleash new levels of performance. The challenge is to take people from a basic level of performance, where simply coming to work and doing the assigned job is sufficient, to a level of performance which is built upon contribution and personal best. The reward shifts from attendance despite effort, to effort despite attendance. The critical dimension is not how long you are at work but what you accomplish. In the past the conventional method of allocating rewards was hours worked or attendance. In the future it will be rewards for contribution, effort and outcomes.

It is a challenge that is less about changing structures and more about changing the relationships. It is less simply directed at changing behaviour and more, as a first step, changing how people think. It involves moving organisations and people from traditional managerial thinking, to that which is required in a highly competitive global marketplace. This is a challenge unlike that which has faced corporate leaders before.

Changes in structure and changes in relationship will occur, but these will flow from the newly emergent ideas about human performance and a rethinking of what constitutes sustainable competitive advantage. Structure and relationships in the past were designed for control, whereas those in the future will be designed to facilitate human development and collaboration and to bring to life the values of the culture. The test will be, do they add value and contribute to the success. If the answer is no, then whatever their merits they will be counterproductive. In a world where the speed of strategic change is increasing rapidly, agility in organisational design and operations will be essential.

The Accelerating Rate of Change

When the rate of change in the external environment is negligible, then "more of the same" as a strategy can work and it can be argued that a managerial mindset which is framed around a drive for consistency, standardisation and predictability, is a sufficient response. When the external environment does not change then today's criteria for success can be replicated into the future.

As the rate of change begins to increase, existing managerial approaches become obsolete and in fact become an impediment to change. Incremental change calls for a process of at least continuous improvement within the organisation and this requires managers to move to more of a coaching paradigm.

When the rate of change becomes extremely rapid and the environment highly turbulent, then even continuous improvement will not keep pace. It is in this environment that the large scale, paradigm shifting approach to change that is termed transformational leadership was introduced. Under this umbrella are grouped concepts such as inspirational leadership, visionary leadership and culture change leadership. However, the two dominant approaches contained within the transformational leadership paradigm, are charismatic leadership and breakthrough leadership. The issue of charisma is well documented within leadership research and leadership theory. Breakthrough leadership is less well understood and is the subject of this research.

The closest parallel to this shake up in management and leadership thinking was probably the challenge facing managers at the onset of the industrial revolution as they took people with an agrarian mindset into the mindset required to work in the new industrial organisations. To some extent there are also parallels with the introduction of scientific management and later with the influence of humanistic psychology.

However, this generation of leaders is faced with unique challenges given the rate of change, the dramatic rise in expectations and the increased complexity of a global economy. The modern era for Western economies really began in the 1980's with concerted international trends towards deregulation, trade liberalisation and the globalisation of financial markets. The competitive imperative was for increased productivity and the central thrust of this was organisational restructuring. The leadership challenge for most was about structure and finding ways to refine it and to improve efficiency. This involved breaking down horizontal and vertical structures and removing layers of hierarchy. The most public impact was large scale retrenchment. I.B.M. in the late 1980's, was one of the best known examples as it retrenched one third of its workforce globally in order to adjust to a dramatically changing strategic landscape where the economic value in that industry was shifting from products to services.

This experience of restructuring quickly led to the realisation that you can't effectively change performance or strategy without a change in culture. Lou Gerstner was the executive who led the culture transformation at I.B.M. and in reflecting upon his experience Gerstner wrote that "I came to see in my time at I.B.M. that culture isn't just one aspect of the game, it is the game". He found that the process was not just about doing things right, but about doing them in a far superior fashion. He observed that for a company to do this however, it requires a commitment from employees that goes far beyond the normal company-employee relationship. Great companies are not just managed but are led by committed, energetic leaders with a passion for winning.

The new century has built on these earlier trends and caused leadership thinking to embrace not only productivity but also performance and agility and flexibility as goals. The objective is now not only to make companies lean and efficient, and not only outward looking and customer centric, but also to bring people to the fore as the primary asset of strategic success. It has produced great interest in the factors which drive human performance and at the same time a strong desire to identify the factors which inhibit human development and performance. It has brought psychology into managerial thinking and sought insights from psychology to better explain human behaviour.

Competitive Advantage Through People

Organisations in the search for the new forms of competitive advantage have turned their attention more to the human element. Whereas organisations once were concerned with manual labour, they became more concerned with human potential. Business leaders have become interested in understanding what people are ultimately capable of. The focus on innovation has produced intense interest in thinking and imagination. The focus on vision has provoked interest in the role of ideas and purpose. Business leaders began to realise that having people come to work and then not accessing what they were truly capable of was a wasted opportunity. The question was raised as to what stopped people from developing at work. The answer all too often was the way they were managed.

This change in emphasis in contemporary leadership thinking and is driven by global leaders looking for ways to achieve significant leaps in performance. Most see this occurring through the process of transforming the nature of their organisations, transforming their relationships and finally transforming the people themselves. This has required a rethinking of change models, of human motivation and psychology and led to great interest in what is now called transformational leadership.

As a concept transformational leadership was first proposed in 1978 by James McGregor Burns in his book "Leadership". As Kenneth and

Miriam Clark explain, "Burn's definition of the transformational leader hinges on the leader's appeal to the loftier ideals of followers rather than to their selfish interests. Transformational leadership is an influence process". In the years that have followed it has become one of the most discussed concepts in leadership theory and practice.

Noel Tichy and Mary Anne Devanna elaborated the concept of transformational leadership. They identified the characteristics of such leaders as:

1. They are agents of change who create adaptive, flexible, entrepreneurial and innovative organisations.
2. They have the courage to take risks and challenge to status quo.
3. They are open with their followers and have confidence in their ability to perform.
4. They have clear values which guide their leadership and their behaviour is consistent with these values.
5. They are committed to life-long learning and continue to adapt as they learn.
6. They are comfortable dealing with complexity and ambiguity.
7. They are visionaries who communicate a vivid picture of the future to their followers.

Tichy and Devanna provided a practical framework for transformational leadership and the special role played by leaders in the transformational process.

This was supported by Bernard Bass and Bruce Avolio who proposed that "an essential distinguishing feature of leaders is their ability to transform followers to perform beyond expectations ... and to move beyond their self-interest to work for the greater good".

They believed that transformational leadership contains four components:

1. Idealised influence
2. Inspirational motivation
3. Intellectual stimulation
4. Individual consideration

Idealised influence is the ability of the leader to be admired and respected by followers. These leaders build trust and become role models for their followers who, over time, adopt some of their behaviours.

Inspirational motivation is the ability of the leader to inspire and motivate the followers to adopt the behaviours necessary to pursue the vision.

Intellectual stimulation is the ability of the leader to encourage followers to challenge old ways of thinking and to be open to new ideas and perspectives.

Individual consideration is the ability of the leader to treat people as individuals and to understand at a deeper level what drives each person.

Bass proposed that "if such transformational leadership is authentic, it is characterised by high moral and ethical standards in each of the above dimensions." He believed that followers identify with these characteristics and seek to emulate these leaders.

Bass concluded that both transformational and transactional styles were important for leaders to use and were in fact complementary approaches deployed depending on the situation or context. For Bass the best of leaders are both transformational and transactional. He believed that transformational leadership enhances the effectiveness of transactional leadership, it does not replace it.

Leadership that Transforms

There is evidence that the physical proximity of the leader has an impact, with transformational approaches being more effective at close range, whilst transactional approaches being more effective at a distance. There is research that has found that "physical distance moderated the effect of transformational leadership on performance". Under close conditions it positively predicted performance, while under distant conditions it did not. This has implication for transformational change in a global context and also for the role of the leader with virtual teams.

A great deal of research interest is also being directed into the character of the transformational leader with researchers such as Jim Collins emphasising the importance of personality variables and especially humility in these leaders. Collins coined the term, "level five leadership" to describe the ultimate stage of leadership development, where leaders are able to balance their fierce determination to win with the humility to understand that you can't do it alone. Both determination and humility are regarded as pre-requisites for success.

Bill George in his book "Authentic Leadership" proposes that leaders become transformational when they themselves are transformed into Authentic Leaders. He observes that "authentic leaders desire to serve others through their leadership. They are more interested in empowering the people they lead to make a difference than they are in power, money or prestige. They are as guided by qualities of the heart, as they are by qualities of the mind. They lead with purpose, meaning and values."

Leaders who are authentic are governed by:

1.   A deep sense of purpose
2.   Values reflected in their behaviours
3.   Compassion
4.   Strong relationships and connection to a common goal
5.   Consistency and self-discipline

Another leadership concept that examines the nature of the leader and is closely related to transformational leadership is the idea of servant leadership. This concept describes the leader as servant first and foremost, and essentially being someone who is working in the service of others. The clear distinguishing characteristic of these leaders is the motivation of the leader.

Servant leadership is primarily associated with the work of Robert Greenleaf, who describes it as a style of leadership whereby the leader's motivation is firstly to serve others and then, and only then, is it permissible to look to one's own needs and interests.

Greenleaf put forward ten characteristics of servant leaders. They are:

1. Listening – they clarify the will of a group by listening receptively to what is being said
2. Empathy – they strive to understand and empathise with others
3. Healing – they have the potential for healing self and others
4. Awareness – that is strengthened by general awareness and self-awareness.
5. Persuasion – they rely on persuasion not positional authority
6. Conceptualisation – they nurture abilities to dream great dreams
7. Foresight – they have the ability to foresee the likely outcome of a situation
8. Stewardship – their first and foremost commitment is to serve others
9. Commitment to the growth of people – they are deeply committed to the growth of others
10. Building community – they seek to build a sense of community in an organisation

These highlight the critical role that trust and service play in the relationship between leader and follower. It is these two which form the basis for the influence that the servant leader has. Servant leadership proposes a fundamental outcome "that those being served grow as individuals, develop talent and become more autonomous".

Robert Greenleaf defines servant leadership as being a servant first and that it begins with the natural feeling that one wants to serve. Conscious choice then brings one to aspire to lead. He believes that this is sharply different from someone who is leader first and foremost and is driven more by some personal need for power. For leaders such as this it will be a later choice to serve – after leadership is established.

The Impact of Transformational Leadership

So, what is it that transformational leaders actually do? How do their behaviours differ from other forms of leadership?

Well known leadership researcher Marshall Sashkin says it is not only what the leader does that is important, but the real impact that the leader has. In a review of the literature on transformational leadership, Sashkin writes that "this type of leadership matters because of the difference it makes. That difference occurs in the lives of followers" and it primarily occurs because "these leaders show that they care about their people" and the outcome is that "they achieve substantially better results, compared to ordinary leaders".

This leads us to the area of the nature and quality of the relationship that the leader has with his or her followers. There is evidence that these leaders spend more time with people than do transactional leaders. Jack Welsh is reported to have spent half his time on employee development. A protégé of his, Lawry Bossidy, wrote that in your career you want to be remembered not for your achievements but rather for how many people you developed.

Part of the leadership challenge today is to understand what leaders actually do. It is more than just their character traits or their guiding principles as leaders. Are their specific, observable behaviours that transformational leaders exhibit in interactions with their followers which produce breakthrough results and enable them to take their performance to a higher level? If we are to truly understand the inspiration that powers the breakthrough experience, it will be necessary to identify the personal behaviour of such leaders and to understand how their behaviour specifically impacts on the mindset of their followers.

Robert Goffee from London Business School has researched the personality that transformational leaders exhibit. He reports that it is more than just self-awareness and being yourself. He writes that it is an "artful authenticity, a deliberate art that leverages their personality characteristics to weld followers to them. They find out which parts of their personality work as leadership tools and amplify them, even if they are weaknesses". The desired outcome he believes is "exciting people to higher performance".

Daniel Goleman who popularised the concept of emotional intelligence focuses on the role of emotion in human performance. He gives a compelling case for the power of the leader's emotion in his book "Working with Emotional Intelligence". Goleman believes that the leader's mood or emotion is contagious and has a powerful impact on the followers' mood and behaviour. Goleman writes of transformational leaders "that they are able to arouse people through the sheer power of their own enthusiasm. They don't order or direct, they inspire. They show strong belief in a vision and excite others about pursuing it with them". He goes on to say that this approach brings greater effort and higher performance.

Today many lenses are being applied to the research into transformational leadership. Some highlight the interaction between leader and follower, others believe the essence is in the personality and belief systems of the leader, whilst others look to how the leader spends his or her time. In all cases what is being explored is the precise nature of inspiration and how it is that people become inspired to achieve more of their potential and in the process become themselves transformed.

Breakthrough leadership in essence is a form of transformational leadership but it is distinctive in that it explains transformation as a process of mindset change. It is more about self-belief and less about motivation, more about removing the impediments to development than finding the right incentives.

The breakthrough leader is concerned with understanding the reasons why people don't develop their full potential at work and sees his or her role as helping people to break through the impediments to their own growth and development. In this way it is a transformational process because it seeks to transform, or fundamentally change how people in the workforce think about themselves, their potential, their contribution and their capability.

For many people the major impediment to their growth is psychological and is due to their own self-limiting thinking. It is less a lack of ability and more a lack of belief in their ability that is the problem. The result is that they might lack the courage or confidence to challenge themselves, and they will tend to undervalue what they are truly capable of. The breakthrough leaders described here exhibit six specific behaviours and display eight leadership attributes which are central to their leadership style.

Chapter 4

What Transformational Leaders Really Do

The psychology of transformation

It is clear that a key lever of transformational leadership is inspiration. The leader's role is to inspire followers to change, to grow, and to develop more of their potential and it is this inspiration that provides the energy and determination necessary to breakthrough habitual and restrictive ways of thinking and behaving. For transformational leaders, inspiration comes primarily from two sources: through charismatic leadership (which inspires through personal example) or breakthrough leadership (which inspires through the relationship). Irrespective of approach or philosophy the intent from an organisational perspective is to produce greater discretionary effort, to achieve greater commitment to the company's goals and to increase the human potential and talent at the company's disposal.

The intent is clear, but what is it that that transformational leaders actually do to inspire? What are the behaviours they exhibit on a day to day basis which has such impact on the people they lead? Identifying the specific behaviours, if there are discrete behaviours, would be of immense value especially to those trying to create competitive advantage through their people. It would also be of great value to those with succession in mind who are intent on grooming the next generation of leaders.

Understanding the behaviours that produce transformation, or at least stimulate the process would give these organisations a sharper focus and a clear agenda from which to work.

If breakthrough behaviours are more a consequence of environmental influence, then they can be targeted directly in leadership development processes. They can also act as a guide for senior leaders, in a mentoring sense, who wish to influence the next generation of leaders through their own personal example. In this way identifying behaviours that can help with the development of people would be of great benefit to organisations, especially those engaged in a highly competitive marketplace where there people with the right skills are scarce.

A great deal of attention has been devoted towards identifying the behaviours that distinguish managers from leaders and those that can differentiate superior leaders from average leaders. What is new is trying to differentiate between transformational leaders and the leaders who are simply seen as good rather than transformational.

Motivating people is not the same as controlling people. It is more concerned with understanding what motivates people and what builds commitment and with understanding how to harness this, direct it and sustain the energy over the long term. Leaders need self-awareness and self-management and skills in building self-esteem, building relationships and influencing others.

Motivating people was not a performance indicator of managers in the past, but it certainly is today a key determinant of effective leadership. With organisations going through constant change, the impact of this over time can test the resilience of even the most determined employee. Sustaining motivation and keeping people energised is today a key leadership responsibility.

John Kotter is an advocate for the proposition that leadership is about inspiring people to achieve more of their potential and that much management behavior does the opposite in inhibiting motivation and inspiration. Kotter takes the view that it is difficult for organisations to produce inspiring leaders because so many of the leaders that new recruits are exposed to at least in the past were such poor role models. His view was that the reality in corporate life, and in careers, was that for most people their work experience was more likely to undermine the development of the attributes required for leadership.

Kotter's solution is the creation of leadership cultures within organisations where new people are exposed to leaders who live and breathe leadership and are powerful role models themselves. He suggests that these exemplar leaders need to be supported by structured processes to identify leadership talents and followed by individual leadership plans for their development.

Looking at the Nature of Transformational Leaders

John Hunt and Bette Laing from London Business School conducted research into the behaviours of what they called exemplar leaders. They used this title to emphasis the characteristics that these leaders displayed as role models to influence others. In their research they reported that the best leaders:

1. Are able to create a sense of vision
2. Have a strong presence and are confident and determined
3. Are action oriented
4. Are role models whose behaviours reflect the values that they espouse
5. Spend more time in face to face communication
6. Are not perfect and selectively display a human frailty or flaw which tends to humanise them

Their behavioural indicators of effective leadership are similar to those proposed by Kotter, with this interesting addition that leaders also need some humanising trait. This is a trait which exposes their humanity rather than portraying them as possessing super human characteristics. They highlighted the character of the leader and the nature of the interaction as being critical to effective leadership.

Robert Goffee also from London Business School has pursued this theme of the allowable flaw in his research. He reported that leaders who inspire do four things:

1. They selectively show their weakness. By exposing some vulnerability they reveal their approachability and humanity.
2. They rely heavily on intuition to gauge the appropriate timing and course of their actions. Their ability to collect and interpret soft data helps them know just when and how to act.
3. They manage employees with something he calls tough empathy. Inspirational leaders empathise passionately - and realistically - with people and they care intensely about the work employees do.
4. They reveal their differences. They capitalise on what is unique about themselves.

Their proposition is that leaders without doubt have to be highly skilled, but they have to be themselves and not try to imitate someone else. If they want to be effective, they need all four of these qualities to be truly transformational. This research emphasises the humanity of the leader, although it is a human leader with a pronounced drive to lead, to achieve and to be successful. So, whilst leaders stand apart in their drive and confidence, it is their basic human qualities which enable them to relate so well to their followers. This is no super human leader, it is leadership which uses the relationship as the basis for inspiration. The skills that the leader needs are those that build relationships and trust and then in order to drive performance and achieve results the leader then uses these skills in the context of the organisational vision and strategy.

Leadership and Transformational Behaviours

Connecting what people do on a daily basis with the organisational vision is a significant strategic leadership challenge. It is clear that leaders need the skills to engage people, what is now becoming clearer are the behaviours that the leaders display in order to align their followers with the strategic goals and vision.

Research today based upon applied global experience is quite specific in relation to the challenges faced by leaders, and quite specific in identifying what it is that make them effective. However, it is clear that this type of research has moved beyond just trying to differentiate between management and leadership and is concerned to understand the social, emotional and psychological impact of leaders on the people that they lead.

Research for the U.K. health Service by Beverley Alimo-Metcalfe and John Alban-Metcalfe identified the factors involved in the transformational process. Their study identified six factors:

1. Valuing individuals (genuine concern for others well being and development)
2. Networking and achieving (inspirational communicator, networker and achiever)
3. Enabling (empowers, delegates, develops potential)
4. Acting with integrity (integrity, consistency, honesty, open)
5. Being accessible (accessible, approachable, in-touch)
6. Being decisive (decisive, risk taking)

This research put the quality of leadership at the heart of the transformational process. What it uncovered was that the quality of the leadership displayed was a mix of character, behaviours and impact factors.

It established that by far and away the most important factor in transformational leadership is valuing individuals and that this has a greater impact than all other factors combined. They reported that, "showing a genuine concern for others is unequivocally the most important aspect of leadership in the U.K. sample explaining more variance than all the remaining factors together".

The U. K. Department of Trade and Industry in 2005, also applied research into organisational effectiveness to learn from the best practices of the leaders in each industry sector. In their publication "Achieving Best Practice In Your Business", they identified the components of outstanding business performance and the attributes of the most successful leaders. Their research gave them clear evidence that an inspired and motivated workforce is essential for any business that hopes to stay ahead of the competition. In an extensive survey of managers, they found that what most wanted most in their leaders was "inspiration".

When they looked further, they identified the characteristics of leaders who inspire as:

- Strong strategic focus
- Lateral thinkers
- Vision and communication
- Principled
- Reflective
- Risk takers
- Accessible
- They value attitude

In this study, they sought not only to describe inspirational leaders, but went further to explore the impact these leaders had on their followers. They were able to draw a direct relationship between the leadership displayed and the resultant impact on followers. They found that leaders who inspire made people feel that they were:

- Being listened to – these leaders asked their people to tell them about how to do things better.
- Being involved – they involved their people in the change process
- Having fun – in successful companies people work hard but enjoy themselves in the process.
- Being trusted – these leaders displayed openness, honesty, respect and trust.
- Being appreciated – they provided recognition and appreciation.
- Being valued – the best build cultures where people understands how their work makes a difference.

This was a significant report because it made clear that leaders for good or bad, have an impact on the people that they lead. It highlighted the importance of the leader's behaviour and it led to the conclusion that if there is a cause and effect between a leader's behaviour and the impact on the follower, then the leader should moderate his or her behaviour according to the desired result the leader is trying to achieve. In other words, leaders to be effective, must control their behaviour and have it essentially guided by the desired outcomes.

This then is the essence of breakthrough leadership. The idea that what leaders do has a discernable impact and is a critical part of the process by which people in a work environment develop their potential and improve their performance.

The Leadership Challenge

Current thinking about leadership behavior and performance has been greatly influenced by the pioneering work of Jim Kouzes and Barry Posner. For over twenty-five years they have explored the "personal best experiences" of leaders and have asked leaders to describe the behaviours that they exhibited when they were able to achieve outstanding results.

They have developed a highly validated and widely used leadership framework described in their best selling book, "The Leadership Challenge".

Their research methodology was to ask leaders to recall a situation where they produced exceptional results. They were then asked to identify what it was they were doing at the time. In other words, in their personal best experience, what were the leadership behaviours that they employed?

They identified what they call the five fundamental practices of exemplary or transformational leadership. They identified these:

1. Challenge the process
2. Inspire shared vision
3. Enable others to act
4. Model the way
5. Encourage the heart

Challenging the process is a combination of searching for opportunities to change the status quo and experimenting and taking risks in order to improve. The research showed that the best leaders are never satisfied with the current state of affairs and are always striving to find a better way

Inspiring a shared vision is the cluster of behaviours that are important once change has been initiated. It is composed of envisioning the future and, through quiet persuasion, enlisting others in that vision. Once the agenda for change has been set it is then critical for leaders to provide focus, and then to get people on board the change. It is not about adopting the leader's vision but building a genuinely shared vision.

Enabling others to act is composed of fostering collaboration, building high performance teams and strengthening the capability of others. Once people have a shared focus the priority then is to equip them with the skills required to be succeed. The best leaders also empower people to be accountable and also build teams to improve performance.

Modelling the way is composed of creating standards of excellence, setting a positive example for others to follow and achieving small wins as they work towards larger objectives. The model of the leader provides a powerful example of what is required and reinforces the commitment of the leader to setting a standard.

Encouraging the heart is composed of recognising individual contributions and celebrating team success. The challenge of sustaining change and performance is daunting one. The best leaders understand that their people need on-going encouragement and recognition if they are to sustain their enthusiasm and effort.

Kouzes and Posner were amongst the first researchers to establish the link between leadership behaviour and team effectiveness. Their work has highlighted the correlation between the practices of leaders and the outcomes for followers. Their model provides an explanatory framework for leadership effectiveness. It starts with challenging the status quo, then inspiring a shared vision, then enabling people to act, all the while modelling the appropriate behaviour and finally providing genuine encouragement along the way.

Although it is a commonly used model for strategic leadership it doesn't really take into account the personal impact of the leader upon the follower. It doesn't offer any insight into how leaders influence the thinking of their followers and enable them to breakthrough beliefs and assumptions which limit their potential and their performance.

Transformation from a European Perspective

A European thought leader with an interest in the nature of the relationship between leaders and followers is Manfred Kets de Vries from INSEAD Business School in France. Kets de Vries combined his training in psycho-analysis with a deep appreciation of organisational dynamics to produce a unique approach to leadership which emphasises psychological factors and interpersonal components of the relationship.

Two academics, Manfred Kets de Vries and Kostantin Korotov, studied the challenges facing European business leaders faced with rapid change and greatly increased expectations. They explained that for leaders to get the best out of their people they must help them deal with the anxieties produced by change and, to do this, leaders need to be skilled at reframing these anxieties as challenges.

They described the universal elements that they believed make leaders able to do this effectively as:

1. Taking time to listen to subordinates and making their opinions count
2. Caring about people and being ready to help them when they have personal problems
3. Setting a good example of what is expected by walking the talk
4. Creating stretch opportunities for people and supporting their personal growth and development
5. Encouraging people by giving them praise and recognition
6. Keeping people informed by creating transparent organisations
7. Setting clear expectations by providing regular feedback
8. Promoting a culture that builds a sense of collective identity
9. Making work meaningful

They went on to describe what is at the heart of the breakthrough experience when people are helped to confront the impediments to their own development. They challenged leaders to help their followers to confront their own fears and anxieties if they want to awaken their potential. They wrote that if leaders want to get the best out of people "they have to create an ambience where their people feel inspired and give their best". This means that their people need "a greater sense of self determination, a feeling of control over their lives" and a "strong belief that their actions are making a difference in their organisations, which can then have an impact upon society at large".

They observed that people also need "a greater sense of competence, a feeling of personal growth and development and, in what they are doing, a feeling of learning new things". They also need "a sense of belonging with being part of an organisation" and they need a "sense of meaning about the activities in which they are engaged".

Kets de Vries and Korotov made the point that it is personal for the leader and that to be effective leaders need a high degree of self-awareness. But it is clearly also personal for the follower and for the process to be effective it is essential that followers also develop a high degree of self-awareness.

Breakthrough leadership is an interactive process between leader and follower where the leader is instrumental in triggering the breakthrough experience for the follower. It is important to understand what the leader does to achieve this result and to identify the specific behaviours that are employed to help followers to confront and overcome the impediments to their development. At the same time, it is equally important to understand what is going on in the mind of the follower and how this drives their resultant behaviour.

Transformational Leadership in Practice

The concept of transformational leadership is quite a complex construct and yet at its essence lies quite a simple proposition: that is that what leaders do actually makes a tangible difference. In other words, the leader has a direct and observable impact on each follower's mindset, behaviour, commitment and ultimately his or her performance. It is something about the leader that inspires others to move from average to exceptional and conversely it is something about the leader which can destroy motivation and undermine aspiration. Leaders can create a better future for their followers, but they can also consign them to a career of frustration and under achievement. As we have seen, there are those who take the view that the drive to unfold potential may be stimulated by the charisma of the leader. A different perspective is that it is more effective and more enduring when it occurs through the relationship with the leader.

It is clear that the leader will have a significant impact on the team and as a consequence that a team's performance will be governed by the quality of leadership which is provided. The strategic drive to boost team performance created great interest in ways to improve the calibre of leadership in teams. This resulted in organisations globally making substantial investments in leadership development and the adoption of highly structured processes for building leadership capability. The focus was increasingly on identifying the behaviours of effective leadership and then putting in place mechanisms to ensure that leaders adopted these behaviours.

The behaviours displayed by leaders are important because not only do they lift the skill levels of professional exchange, but they are also a reflection of the values and mindset of the leader concerned. Followers are directly affected by the professional skill of the leader. Leaders who have well developed communication skills and coaching skills can be highly effective at engaging their followers and in developing their capability. They build in their followers a real sense of confidence, confidence in themselves and confidence in their leaders.

The leader's behaviour also has a less tangible influence upon others, but one that is equally as important. When followers observe their leaders, they also make judgements about what the leader's priorities are and what they really care about. People observe behaviour and then infer values and, because leaders are always on display and people are always watching what they do, they are always making judgements about their leader's motives. When there is consistency between the values espoused and the behaviours experienced, this builds trust. When there is a discrepancy between the two, the result is increased cynicism.

Making leaders aware of the impact of their behaviour is the essence of self-awareness. Ensuring that leaders have the discipline to control their behaviour requires self -management. Self-awareness and self-management are the building blocks of effective leadership. These form the foundations upon which the skills needed to build trust, drive performance and develop potential are established. These skills form the nucleus of breakthrough leadership.

Chapter 5

Breakthrough Leadership

The breakthrough leadership research

Whilst a great deal has been written about charismatic leadership and there are scores of biographies of charismatic leaders, less has been written about the behaviours that define breakthrough leadership. It is this breakthrough experience which is the focus of the research described in this book.

This research sets out to fill that gap and to explore the defining moments in people's lives when they took a step up in their development. A principle objective was to look at leaders who had inspired people to achieve more of their potential and to discover what it was that these leaders did. Another objective was to get a better understanding of the breakthrough experience and a third was to look at the nature of the leaders themselves.

What the Research set out to do?

This research set out to answer three questions:

1. What are the behaviours that breakthrough leaders exhibit?
2. What impact do breakthrough leaders have on their followers?
3. Are there certain attributes displayed by breakthrough leaders?

Over eight hundred managers were involved in this research. They were mostly middle to senior level managers attending leadership and executive programs at Mt Eliza Business School in Australia during the period from 1999-2010.

This research sought to identify specific situations where participants reported that they were inspired to meet a challenge and went on to achieve more of their potential. Information was gathered through experiential exercises where participants were asked to identify specific breakthrough experiences in their careers and to reflect upon the leaders involved and the nature of the interaction.

Specifically, participants were asked to think about a time in their careers when a manager had inspired them to move to a higher level of functioning. They were asked to think about leaders who had had a significant impact on them, and to recall the situations when this occurred. They were asked to recall the leaders who had inspired them and this was defined as leaders who:

1. saw the potential in them that perhaps even they didn't see
2. gave them a challenge and the courage to meet it
3. were instrumental in moving their career to a higher level
4. gave them the confidence to face self-doubt
5. gave them greater belief in their own potential and lifted their aspirations and expectations

They were then asked to go into small teams, tell the stories in detail of how they were inspired and then as a team, compile a list of behaviours that were common to the leaders in each situation. The second part of the exercise was to consider the impact upon them of the leader and the leader's specific behaviour. In other words, how did the leader make them feel, think or behave?

In summary the exercise was:

> First identify a time when you were inspired and tell your story to the others in your team. Describe the interaction with your leader. Identify exactly what the leader concerned did.

> Next discuss these examples to identify any behaviours consistently displayed by the leaders.

> Then discuss the impact the leaders had on their followers in terms of "thinking" and "feeling".

> The last part of the exercise was for teams to discuss the attributes and characteristic of these leaders.

The Research Findings

What emerged from the team discussions was highly consistent. A clear pattern of behaviour exhibited by the leaders identified was described and the impact upon followers was similarly consistent. Six practices emerged that were common themes in almost all stories.

What leaders did that inspired was:

1. They showed a genuine interest in each person's development
2. They listened and asked for ideas
3. They acted on advice
4. They set a challenge and showed confidence in their ability
5. They provided support and coaching
6. They gave feedback and recognition

The leadership practice which emerged most consistently in the responses was one which I describe as the leader showing a genuine interest in their follower's development. In 91% of the discussions about what leaders did that inspired them, words, examples or phrases were used which reflected this practice. The second most commonly attributed practice was when leaders provided feedback and recognition. This was reflected in 89% of the examples given. Acting on advice was rated important in 80% of cases, listening was featured in 88% of examples, providing support in 87% examples and setting a challenge in 85% of examples given.

These were the themes or behaviours which were most commonly featured. Other behaviours which were often identified were those such as "builds trust", "sets a strong personal example", "has clear expectations", "wouldn't take no for an answer", "set very high standards", "gave you the time and the space to perform", and "created a strong team environment". Whilst there were a range of responses and a variety of interpretations none had the same frequency as the leadership practices identified.

1. Shows a genuine interest in my development

Whilst the words and phrases used varied across individuals, workplaces and even countries, the meaning was remarkably consistent. It was clear that the foundation for breakthrough was a leader who showed a genuine interest in the development of each individual follower. These leaders put in the time required to gain a deeper understanding of the psychology of each follower, and to appreciate what motivates and drives what they do. Showing a genuine interest cannot be superficial, nor can it be conducted in haste. It is a real commitment from the leader as part of his or her professional responsibility to those being led. It takes time to build trust in a relationship and it is only through the establishment of trust that a follower in particular will be open with the leader and open to the leader's influence.

Fiona, a 35 year old sales team leader in an international company said that the leader who had inspired her most was someone who "gave me the time".

"He gave me time that was solely for me, without interruptions. Although he was busy and we were under a lot of pressure to hit our targets, he never seemed hurried or put me off. When it was my time, he was there for me. He made me feel that, at that moment, I was the most important item on the agenda".

Greg, a 42 year old finance manager in the automotive sector: expressed gratitude for a leader who had "taken a personal interest in me and in my career".

"I had known him for some time before he became my manager and he had always been friendly and asked how I was. When I moved into his department, I had no hesitation as I felt that we already had a good rapport. At our first formal meeting he was asking me about my expectations and my career aspirations and he has continued that on".

Other respondents spoke about the sincerity of their manager. George, a 33 year old accounts team leader in a pharmaceutical company:

"I met him first when he interviewed me for the job. I almost felt that I was interviewing him because he was very interested in my expectations and he was very interested in how I thought I could make a contribution. He has this strong belief. It's not just the results you deliver, it's also how well you are developing in your job".

Some respondents felt that they never before had a manager "who was so friendly and interested in me as a person". Sam, a 38 year old technical specialist from a funds management group:

"He is a leader I really admire. He puts in time and he has a way of making everyone on the team feel valued. With him it's personal – you really feel that he's not just doing his job. He seems to care about the relationship".

Often respondents would identify the leader as "more like a mentor, not like a boss at all". These were leaders that their followers looked up to and respected, and there was clearly an emotional connection whereby there seemed to be some reciprocal attraction. It was apparent that these leaders understood that part of their leadership role was to develop their people and to help them achieve their career potential. It wasn't simply a friendship, although these leaders were friendly. It was more that they needed to understand each person sufficiently in order to build an effective working relationship and to understand their unique psychology.

Putting in time meant being available and accessible. Many leaders with busy lives run out of time to devote to their people. It is a fundamental of breakthrough leadership, however, that leaders make it a high priority to spend regular quality time with each person that they lead. People are often reluctant to ask for help from leaders who appear too busy, not wanting to place a greater burden on them. Leaders who place a high priority on the development of their people make sure that time is set aside continually to build and deepen the relationship with each follower. This step is the bottom line which builds the foundations for the transformational process.

2. Listens and asks for ideas

Listens was often associated with asking for advice and breakthrough leaders were invariably described as good listeners. "Gave me individual attention" was a phrase commonly used to describe them. Many leaders are too distracted to give their followers undivided attention. They are often pre-occupied with demands from their own bosses, or competing demands for attention from a range of followers, or with managing the expectations of multiple stakeholders. Being able to shut out distracting thoughts and being at one with the person in the moment is the making of an exceptional leader.

But it is not just listening which is the key – it is also asking for ideas and welcoming contributions. This is an extension of showing a genuine interest and the follower can gauge from the questions asked and from the body language displayed the extent to which the interest is genuine.

Many respondents expressed the view "that the leader was always interested in what I thought". Sarah, a 45 year old corporate lawyer in investment banking:

"She is always running things by me, asking me about how I read something. She really tries to involve you in the process and she makes you feels that your opinions are important. She is prepared to challenge and she likes it when I push back. She is really stimulated by the debate and I find that she makes me think deeper about an issue".

Others expressed that it was "corridor conversations, conducted on the run". Tom, a 36 year old engineer in the mining sector:

"He always picks the right moment, but sometimes gets you on the hop. It will be in the corridor and he'll see you coming and want to know what you think. Sometimes I feel unprepared but he's always happy for me to come back when I've had a chance to gather my thoughts properly. It's just the way he is, he is very excited about ideas and very excited about getting your thoughts".

Julie, a 34 year old sales administrator in an internet company said her leader was "always interested in what people thought especially in our team meetings".

"He is great at team meetings. He goes around the room and draws people in. It's impossible not to have an opinion, not to contribute. We really find out where people stand and it gives you a great sense of team cohesion. I have learnt a lot from him and I am sure everyone in the team feels more confident and capable. I really look forward to our meetings".

These leaders asked questions, reflected and stimulated discussion and debate. It was observed that they did this "in order to get us to think more deeply about an issue and in a way, they were better able to influence us as a team". The ability to ask questions seemed to be a reflection of the leader's curiosity but also in a subtle way, it was a powerful influencing technique. These leaders displayed a desire to know more, and showed that they valued the other person's point of view. They were seen as being open. The ability to listen was the characteristic with the second highest frequency of response.

It was not really surprising the high rating given to the ability to listen. What differentiated the breakthrough leaders, however, was their ability to move beyond simple listening to the use of listening as a mechanism for engagement and influence. These were leaders who through the use of insightful questions would also score high on perceptions of empathy.

3. Acting on advice

Breakthrough leaders were also good at acting on advice. In this way they could show that not only were they interested in gathering opinions and understanding different perspectives, but that they were also capable of being influenced. This is a very strong involvement technique and it is a way that these leaders get genuine buy in to new ideas.

Acting on advice is an important technique in change management to generate ownership for initiatives or processes and is an essential part of any empowerment process. Listening and asking for new ideas gives these leaders a chance to frame the debate and to influence thinking and as a consequence, it becomes less of a risk to act on advice received.

Through the relationship established, the leader also has an understanding of how each follower thinks and how they are likely to react in the event of a crisis or a particular challenge. This understanding, gives the leader the ability to relate the degree of empowerment given to the level of confidence and capability of each follower.

Frequently, respondents commented that the leader "really empowered me and expressed the confidence that I could do the job well". Paul, a 40 year old human resource manager in the retail sector:

"He is such a good leader. The last one I had was a bit of a bureaucrat and was only interested in getting the right procedures in place. He is different. He really gives me the feeling that it's my call and for the first time I really think I can make an impact in this department".

A common view was that "the leader trusted me and believed that I knew what to do". Trust and empowerment were common themes and acting on advice was often interpreted as an indicator of trust and a measure of empowerment.

These leaders were open to ideas and opinions and some respondents expressed this as "asking for suggestions and then taking them on board".

Susan, a 52 year old general manager in a bank:

"John is an excellent executive and he has made such a difference to the leadership team. He listens, asks questions and then initiates action if the business case has been made. On issues where there is a need for group consensus from all departments, he will act on advice if there is unanimous support. He will not accept second best though and our meetings will go until he believes that the issues have been brought out and resolved. I feel that I can challenge and have my say – it really encourages contribution".

Some commented that they saw how "I could have an impact and where I could really influence what happened". Mary, a 35 year old human resource manager in an international company:

"I was new in the job, and a little anxious, because it was a big step up for me and a totally new industry. She was very helpful and helped me through a steep learning curve. What I appreciated was that she was looking for new ideas and was very open to my point of view. It was just such a refreshing experience to see that I could make a difference".

Acting on advice is a key part of passing the baton to a new generation of leaders. The leader, of course must be flexible enough to know that there are many ways to solve problems and a range of ways to manage any situation. Leaders who are high on control and want things done their way, find this step to be very challenging. It requires the maturity of a leader who can define parameters, clarify objectives and then leave it up to the followers to determine the method or the approach. In simple terms the leader explains the why, the follower determines the how.

These leaders were judged to be collaborative and prepared to look at different ways of doing things. They were prepared to be flexible with processes and systems and this led to delegation and greater genuine empowerment. Being empowered was seen as a vote of confidence by the leader in the capability and commitment of the follower. Empowering people requires a great deal of trust that they will deliver.

Astute leaders whilst empowering people will still monitor progress at arm's length. Not too close so that it gives any hint of micro-management, yet not so far that it is seen as an abrogation of any responsibility by the leader. The ability to set the right degree of freedom for each follower is an appropriate management of risk, balanced by the extent of confidence in the follower's ability to deliver.

4. Sets a challenge and shows confidence in a person's ability to achieve it

The ability to set an appropriate, effective challenge is a key developmental strategy for the breakthrough leader. Too great a challenge is daunting, too small a challenge is not really motivational. The degree of stretch is the critical ingredient in the developmental mix. It is the confidence that is generated by the high-level involvement of the leader, and the trust built through the personal relationship, that enables the follower to take on a significant degree of stretch.

Feedback from the respondents indicated that more stretch was a better challenge than too little and far more motivating. They also indicated that quite a lot of the development required to meet the challenge was gained through the assignment itself and not prior. The development required to enable followers to breakthrough old ways of thinking was contained within the challenge itself. What it needed was the confidence to step up, and the courage to confront the risk of failure.

Respondents often remarked that the leader "never seemed to be in any doubt that I could do it". Jane, a 37 year old merchandising manager in the retail sector:

"He always makes you feel that you can do more, that there is more you can achieve. He will just give me that challenge and then expect that I can do it. He has great confidence even when I'm not too sure that I can do it. It gives me confidence to know that I have his confidence, but even more, that I have his support when things aren't going well".

Many commented that the leader always seemed to be looking for the next challenge for them and once this was decided "then let me get on with it, in my own way". Henry, a 35 year old corporate lawyer in a government enterprise:

"What I really liked about him was that he let me do it my way. A lot of lawyers want briefs written their way and can be highly critical. He will give constructive advice and seek clarification, and suggest improvements, but in the end, he is happy for me to use my own style and judgement".

These leaders seemed to have the ability to present challenges in the most exciting way, articulating the benefits and endorsing the opportunity. One respondent described the leader as someone "who always took the positive view and could sell the opportunity".

Being able to present the challenge in a persuasive way and making it personally relevant to the development of each person, is a powerful leadership technique. Expressing confidence in a person's ability to meet a challenge is a strong endorsement of untapped potential and is a recognition of a person's aptitude to learn and to perform.

These leaders looked for challenges for their followers and created opportunities where they would be stretched. Often these leaders had to be confident even in the absence of confidence from their followers. Without doubt they gave followers a belief that they could genuinely "make a difference". Whether or not the leaders in their own minds always felt confident that their followers could rise to the challenge is unclear. What is clear is that they never gave their followers any hint of reservation.

Despite their confidence they were never so blasé that they totally discounted any risks involved. They were never described as foolhardy, but as leaders who had a deep and genuine belief in their follower's ability to step up and to meet a challenge and to deliver. Perhaps a key quality that differentiates breakthrough leaders is their ability to gauge potential and see what might be possible. Perhaps it is a combination of optimism and vision that gives these leaders such apparent confidence. Perhaps it is also the ability to select the appropriate challenge. Whatever it is the leaders described were able to identify the next step for their followers in order to continue their growth and development.

5. Coaches and provides support

Breakthrough leaders are adept at providing the support required for their followers to accept challenges. By putting in place a safety net they give their followers the courage to step out of a comfort zone and accept a degree of risk that would otherwise be too daunting.

Their quiet reassurance and the availability of a helping hand, if required, enabled even tentative followers to deal with the anxiety provoked when stepping out of familiar territory into the unknown. It meant that the anxiety did not become debilitating and a major impediment to change.

Being prepared to coach ensures that followers can build skills and capabilities which become real assets for their own development.

Through the coaching process it is clear that many leaders deepen and consolidate their relationship with their followers and increase their impact and their influence. This hands-on leadership is a major avenue for passing on knowledge and experience and is a significant investment in building future organizational capability.

Most respondents noted that their leader was "always there when needed". James, a 28 year old team leader in a media firm:

"She is very hands on – but in a helpful way. She gives me the targets and then we talk through what I will do to achieve them. She gives me a lot of support with my team and because she has been in my situation, she has a good understanding of how to motivate people and how to deal with difficult people. If I have to have a particularly difficult conversation with a member of the team, I always run it by her for her advice".

Some respondents commented that the leader "always seemed to know when I need help". Sarah, a 44 year old manager in a pharmaceutical company:

"He doesn't micro-manage but he seems to have a good idea about what is happening. We meet regularly and it's great to bounce ideas around so that

I can get a different perspective. He loves to be provocative and at times I think he does it just to get a reaction from me. The most important thing for me is that he supports me but gives me the freedom to do it my way".

Importantly leaders did not remove the challenge if the follower ran into trouble, knowing that to do so would undermine the confidence generating by the preceding steps. One respondent expressed gratitude that the leader "didn't take it back when I ran into trouble". Another said that the leader "didn't falter in her belief and confidence that I could handle the project even at times when I began to have doubts myself".

Successfully mastering a challenge is the best way to build a track record of achievement which can accelerate career progression. If one thing stood out it was that the leaders put in the time required to coach and support and to help their followers build their own capabilities and confidence. These leaders were seen as coaches in their own right. Support is a very personal thing. Too much or too little can both be a problem at times. The support must be geared to the psychological maturity of each follower and given in a way that reinforces self-esteem rather than diminishes it.

Coaching is a fundamental skill of breakthrough leaders and it is one that directly enables them to build capability. It is hands on, practical and action oriented, and it is a skill that makes a direct investment in the future potential and future contribution of each follower. Confidence comes not just through psychological factors, but also increased capability.

Both capability and confidence come together in a virtuous circle to boost performance and to increase achievement. Greater ability gives rise to greater confidence, which allows greater challenge and produces greater results. The process itself can become self-sustaining with the leader monitoring where, and how much intervention might be required.

6. Gives feedback and recognition

Finally, breakthrough leaders know that recognition is one of the most powerful motivational tools available to them. They know that many people fail to shine in because their efforts are not appreciated and that many leave organisations because they feel unwanted. Attention and appreciation are important needs built into the human psyche. They generate a sense of significance that builds self-worth and a sense of mastery that gives people confidence about their contribution.

Instilling a belief in people that they can make a difference brings meaning to their work and a sense of importance to their role. Many respondents were particularly struck by the care their leaders placed on providing recognition. Typical comments included that "he always made sure that we knew our work was appreciated". Tim, a 44 year old account executive in a real estate and property development firm:

"He is such a great leader. He always walks around the office each morning to talk to the people. A lot of other managers lock themselves away and you hardly see them. He makes people feel appreciated. It is always interested in what is happening and what you are doing. He makes you feel encourages because he gives you recognition".

Others commented that the leader "was excellent at putting the spotlight on us". John, a 35 year old marketing manager in the automotive industry:

"We have put a lot of work into this branding exercise and the launch went really well. He didn't try to take the credit – he was happy that we received the recognition. I know that this is just the first step and that there is a lot more work to be done, but the exercise has really lifted the confidence of the whole team".

These leaders see that giving feedback is a form of recognition, and is a key tool within a coaching repertoire. They are prepared to be honest and direct but to do so in a way that is respectful of the person. Tough feedback is given privately and feedback that can be placed within a more general learning context is often given more openly in a team.

Many leaders dodge tough feedback and would prefer to reassure than to challenge. Breakthrough leaders are candid but they do so with care, and in this way their followers know where they stand and they know that if there is an issue it will be raised directly with them. In this way they know there will be no secrets and they can trust that there will be no hidden agendas. Concerns about hidden agendas undermine trust and raise doubts about the sincerity of interactions.

The breakthrough leaders clearly knew the difference between feedback and criticism. They were able to give constructive feedback in a way that did not make followers feel criticised. This is an essential element in any development process because criticism undermines self-confidence and attacks self-esteem. This in turn leads to defensive behaviour on the part of the follower.

Breakthrough leaders are able to keep their followers responsive to feedback and open to influence by the way in which they use both recognition and feedback. Poor leaders on the other hand put a distance between themselves and their followers by the overuse of criticism as a corrective mechanism. Unfortunately, respondents in this research reported that they were exposed overall to more poor leaders in the workplace than breakthrough ones. However, most were able to identify enough of the latter who at critical stages in their careers made a real difference in what they achieved.

When the small groups met to discuss their stories and to reflect upon the impact that these leaders had, it was clear that in these breakthrough experiences the leaders had an influence in how the respondents felt about themselves and their potential. The followers described variously feeling more valued, more important, more powerful, more committed, more courageous and more appreciated. The words were not always the same but the emotional impact was consistent and clear.

In these breakthrough situations the respondents felt:

1. Valued

They felt that they mattered. Many commented that poor leaders make you feel that you don't matter by ignoring you. When a leader shows a genuine personal interest in you, you feel that you have some significance as a human being. To devalue a person is to negate their potential and to minimise their possible contribution. It is an assault upon a person's self-esteem. When a person feels valued, it reinforces their self-worth and their confidence.

The breakthrough leaders identified here made significant investments in the self-esteem of their followers by showing an interest in them that was personal and genuine. A strong self-esteem is necessary for building the confidence in followers that they have greater ability than they currently display and greater potential than they currently think.

2. Important

They felt that they were important in the scheme of things. When a leader asks for ideas or suggestions it makes people feel that their opinions count. It gives them the feeling that their ideas and experience have some worth. In contrast poor leaders discount the contribution of followers and are not open to being influenced. A leader with a closed mind leaves little scope for individual initiative. This often stems from the arrogance of leaders who think they know better, or the lack of interest from leaders who don't really care.

Breakthrough leaders appreciate that when people feel important, it lifts their pride and their engagement. In the same way when people don't feel important, they experience a sense of loss and they become disengaged as a way of protecting their self-esteem. Feeling important is a powerful indicator of self-worth and is itself a motivator towards greater achievement.

3. Powerful

They felt that they could influence events. When a leader shows a follower how their ideas can influence outcomes, it generates a tremendous sense of empowerment. Poor leaders on the other hand keep control for themselves, and the most controlling leaders micro-manage and stifle the development of others.

Breakthrough leaders empower their followers to bring their own style to their work. They manage risk by establishing clear goals and parameters and by holding people accountable for achieving goals within those parameters. People who feel powerful have a belief in their ability to influence outcomes. They possess what is referred to as an internal locus of control, whereby they believe that what happens to them is a consequence of their own actions and they are more likely to use their initiative and to be pro-active. A person with an external locus of control is more passive and believes, on the other hand, that what happens to them is due to external forces or fate or luck. Leaders can have a great influence on whether their followers develop an internal or external locus of control.

4. Commitment

They felt that the confidence that was shown in them had to be returned – it was in this way a form of mutual obligation. When a leader trusts a follower to perform, it generates feelings of responsibility, of having to live up to expectations. Poor leaders never get the same sense of commitment because they never truly trust the other to deliver. Often the low expectations exhibited generate a low performance outcome in return, because living up to expectations doesn't deliver much, when the expectations are low to begin with. This commitment becomes a deeper conviction when the leaders create a compelling vision and a sense of purpose for the work.

Breakthrough leaders bring significance to work and build the conviction that what one is doing is truly worthwhile. This then becomes a powerful source of intrinsic motivation. It is intrinsic motivation that produces change that is self-sustaining, because it is derived from personal measures of satisfaction rather the externally determined measures of worth.

5. Courage

They felt more courageous when a safety net was in place. When a leader provides support and coaching to followers it gives them a great deal more confidence to accept a challenge, and builds the courage to step out of their comfort zones. Challenging the status quo can cause great anxiety and a leader needs to be aware of this and provide the reassurance needed to ensure that anxiety doesn't become debilitating. Anxiety can undermine motivation and stress can certainly lead to a decline in performance.

Breakthrough leaders provide the care and support that most people need when dealing with situations that are challenging and confronting. It is the courage to take a risk and to confront a challenge that becomes personally liberating for followers. This is especially true for those who in the past have been frightened of showing their vulnerability or have experienced strong fear of failure.

6. Appreciated

Nothing warms the human heart quite like appreciation. When a leader says "thanks" it has a powerful motivating affect upon the follower. Poor leaders show lower levels of appreciation and give less feedback to their followers. This is not necessarily due to a lack of appreciation, often it is because of a lack of thought or awareness of its potential impact. Many successful leaders have very strong self-esteem and seem not to require much appreciation or feedback themselves and so don't see the need to give much out.

Breakthrough leaders are aware of the power of recognition, and use it effectively to motivate and to drive ownership of tasks. The recognition doesn't need to be extreme, and when it simply comes in personal appreciation, it often has the greatest impact.

The important thing about recognition is that it has to be genuine. Recognition that is insincere or inappropriate can have the opposite effect and lead to disengagement and disenchantment. Recognition also needs to be expressed in ways that culturally appropriate. There are cultures where ostentatious displays of appreciation are normal parts of daily life, and other cultures where being set apart from the team would be embarrassing for all concerned.

It is clear that the breakthrough leaders identified had a strong impact. They gave people greater self-assurance, confidence and courage to pursue their dreams. They also generated a sense of expectation and even obligation – "he had such confidence in me I felt obliged to follow through"; "I didn't want to let her down"; "I felt committed"; "I felt a debt I had to repay"; "he had such trust in me I felt in a way as if I had no choice". It wasn't just that these leaders provided support, it was also that they raised expectations and increased accountability.

Over and again respondents recalled the influence that these leaders had had on their lives. For most, these situations could be easily recalled and for many the emotions felt were still close to the surface. It is clear that there is a strong emotional component to the breakthrough experience. The link between the leader's behaviour and the feelings generated is strong and is clearly an important part of the breakthrough experience. This experience has both a cognitive and an affective element. It changed how respondents thought and felt about themselves and their potential.

Participants could see in their own experience that if you want people to feel valued, important, powerful, confident, appreciated and with a sense of commitment to perform, then there are certain leadership behaviours that are more likely to be productive and others that are not. Poor leaders are likely to produce followers who feel less significant and less empowered and as a consequence they will be less likely to challenge themselves and to challenge the status quo.

What emerged also was that whilst such inspirational situations were common to all, they were by no means common. They were rare or at best infrequent events, but events that had a huge impact. Most could identify one or two situations in a career. Some could not recall a single moment when they had been inspired. A few said that they learnt more from bad leaders about what not to do.

The stories told provided a powerful testament to the impact that leaders have on the lives of the people they lead. What was sobering was that this was not a part of daily leadership practice. The opportunity to be grasped is to make it a regular occurrence, a part of daily managerial life. It is breath-taking to speculate what might be achieved if leaders at all levels made it a priority to develop their followers and to inspire them to achieve their potential. It would be truly transformational if all leaders were to do this as part of their professional practice on a regular and personal basis.

The participants in these exercises were clear about the impact specific leaders had had on them. They expressed a great sense of gratitude to the leaders who had made such a profound difference to their careers and their lives They could then appreciate the impact that they as leaders were having on their followers. This led to many "a ha" experiences as they could see the power of this in transformational change especially if it were to be regular, personal, and purposefully developmental.

They could also appreciate where the impact that they were having might not be what they desired. It proved to be a powerful experience grounded in their own emotional reactions to leaders. It was an experience which they could translate easily into experience with their own direct reports.

Chapter 6

The Practices of Breakthrough Leaders

The six behaviours in detail

Most of us can recall the people in our lives who have had a significant impact on our development. It might be a school teacher who was passionate about mathematics who inspired us to believe that we too could embrace numbers. Often it is parents who have left an indelible imprint in our personalities and mindsets through explanations or their own philosophies. It could be the sporting coach who saw the potential and provided the motivation and support the individual needed to put in the hours of training required.

With these people, most of us can recall specific situations that might be called defining moments where decisions were made, where motivation was found, expectations were raised and the courage to confront a particular challenge was called for. In hindsight it can be seen that these defining moments have a significant impact on personal development and future outcomes. Invariably it was the right person in the right place at the right time. Often it is hard to appreciate the significance of these events at the time. Usually there is a mix of emotion. Fear and anxiety mixed with aspiration and excitement. But it is in hindsight that these can be seen as defining moments.

Just as the key people in our personal lives have such a significant impact, so too do the managers, the mentors, the bosses, the leaders that we encounter in our working lives. When prompted people can easily identify the times and places, and the leaders who helped them along the way. Those who were fortunate found someone early in a career who inspired and really supported their career development. These were in fact breakthrough leaders – leaders who worked in the realm of mindset change.

In an interesting parallel to this research, Teresa Amabile, Professor of Management from Harvard University, has looked at how leaders create the conditions for creativity and innovation to be developed and especially the behaviours that they exhibit. She writes that "the researchers were struck by the profound ways in which a manager's ordinary, routine interactions with subordinates can support – or undermine – innovation. ...it was a process whereby seemingly trivial behaviours engaged in on a day to day basis would have profound indirect influence". They found that leader support was a critical variable and they outlined four key leadership behaviours which provided that support.

1. Monitoring which was over viewing, not undermining, the subordinate's autonomy
2. Consulting which was being open to the subordinate's ideas
3. Supporting which was managing stress and keeping people informed
4. Recognising which was showing empathy and providing recognition

She says that people don't want leaders to get out of their way. What they want is leaders who are consultative and provide arms-length support. This is similar to what we discovered about breakthrough leaders. People are looking for leaders to inspire them and instead what they all too often get are leaders who just want to control them. We found that people are grateful to the leaders who help them, and profoundly thankful to those who inspired them to do their best. The leadership behaviours uncovered by Amabile and her team are almost identical to the breakthrough behaviours we found.

Patricia Wallington, writing in C.I.O. Magazine, vividly described her experience with an inspirational leader:

"First he was always accessible. No matter how busy he was, he made time for me. To me, it meant I mattered. Second, he never solved my problems. Instead, he gave me guidance in the form of principles that could be used over and over again for different situations. Third, he encouraged me by praising my strengths. It was up to me to use them to succeed. Last, and maybe most important, he "lifted me up". He made me feel I could do anything. Isn't that what inspiration is all about."

Just like Patricia, when managers are asked to identify these people, they can and often in vivid detail. The behaviors recalled consistently show a strong relationship to the breakthrough behaviours.

1. Shows a genuine interest in my development

It is inconceivable that you could inspire someone that you are disinterested in, that you spent little time with and gave no encouragement to. It doesn't mean that you have to be particularly friendly with the person, or even that you need to like them. These things help of course and make it easier to put in the time and establish the intimacy required to achieve deeper understanding of the person's psychology. In this context it is clearly a professional responsibility of all leaders to develop people.

It is much like the coach of a football team whose job it is to get the best out of each player and to find the way to help them to play effectively as part of the team. The coach is a professional. The coach may not like all the players but nevertheless it is his or her responsibility to develop their potential and find ways for them to work as part of a team. Often the coach is dealing with strong egos, with highly strung temperaments and with conflicting emotions, but the task is clear. It is to find the way to help each player to be a better contributor and performer for the team. The objective is also clear and that is to win the game being played.

The leader of a team in business is also in a similar situation. It is often with a team of diverse talents that the leader is charged with achieving important business results. In this highly competitive global marketplace, this usually means achieving what are termed stretch goals. The rate of change means that leaders don't have the long timeframes that were more a feature of past managerial life.

Incremental change is rarely an option. The increased expectations from a range of stakeholders also means that accountability for results is being pushed down to frontline teams across the business.

All of this means that business leaders at all levels have to be more like the coach. They have to see it as their job to get the best out of each player or team member. It is a leadership challenge, one to one, to make each member of the team the best they can be.

Adding to the pressure is what has been referred to as the war for talent. This is described as the problem of finding, in what is a global talent shortage, enough of the right people to do the job. In addition, all of this must be done within what is referred to as "a salary cap". No one can just put more players in the team, more players on the field. In all spheres we are constrained by salary costs. The only option is to get more out of the people we have, to develop more of each person's potential.

Marcus Buckingham and Curt Coffman in their review of research by the Gallop Organisation put it this way:

"Companies are searching for undiscovered reserves of value. Human nature is one of those last, vast reserves of value….its power lies in the fact that each human's nature is different. If companies want to use this power, they must find a medicine to unleash each human's nature, not contain it. You, the manager, are the best medicine they have."

The leader's role is to bring out the best in people and the challenge is to do this person by person. This is about psychology not structure, it is more about mindset change, less about skills development. The starting point is to show a genuine interest in the development of each person. The key point is that it must be genuine. People can smell insincerity and mistrust. This is not about whether a person is perceived to be worthwhile or not. It is about the leader's commitment to work with each person to help him or her to be more effective, and to find a way to help them to make a greater contribution, to create more value in their own personal way. Simply put, the challenge is to make each person more valuable in the work they do and in the contribution they make.

It is less about personal preference, and more about professional discipline. The leader needs an individual target and approach for each person, and needs to find the trigger to move each one forward. To do this the leader needs to understand each person's unique psychology and what holds them back and what moves them forward.

The best leaders in this research were firm but fair and were seen as unrelenting in their belief in the greater potential each person possessed.

The best way to make another person feel valued is to show a genuine interest in his or her development. The leaders who do this well, do so as a matter of personal discipline, and they view it as their professional responsibility. Amongst a range of things that they do there are three key practices.

These are:

    (a) making a regular time to talk with the individuals in the team
    (b) showing a real interest in what they are doing
    (c) displaying an understanding of their needs

There is variability according to individual style as to how these practices are demonstrated, but the key is that they are part of a leader's regular practice. They are made a priority, the time is allocated and there is follow through. There is no substitute for personal contact in building a relationship and they need continual nurturing in order to be sustained. It is very easy to lose touch through absence and reduce intimacy through neglect.

2. Listens and asks for ideas

Good leaders are essentially good listeners first. There are a number of specific things that a leader does in that process. First of all, a good leader listens and learns.

It is not just a matter of listening to another person to hear what they say, it is more a matter of listening to hear what they think. It is a basic way that we as humans show respect for another person in that we take the time to listen to what they have to say.

The inspirational leaders will then take the time and show the interest to ask questions in order to get a clearer understanding of what the person thinks, what evidence their assumptions are based on and what level of aspiration or motivation the person possesses. The leader asks questions not only to get greater understanding, but also because it helps the other person to think, to clarify their thoughts and to reach conclusions.

This skill is called active listening and is used to pick up verbal and non-verbal cues, and is used to understand both cognitive (thoughts) as well as emotional (feeling) content.

David Maister and Patrick McKenna in "First among Equals" describe it as "a technique that reduces defensiveness and makes people feel that they are being understood. This frees them to explore their own feelings, to express their ideas and to rely less on defensive behaviour".

The participants in this research report that when their leaders listen to them and then ask for their ideas, they feel a great sense of importance and it is this sense of importance that builds confidence and gives the person a belief that their ideas and feelings are worthwhile. This encourages them to speak up and to feel that they have something of value to contribute.

The skillful leader through thoughtful questions can help the other to think through issues, see things from a different perspective and to challenge old ways of thinking and seeing the world. A good question is one which causes the other to pause, to reflect more deeply and to critically appraise their thoughts and responses. This leader appreciates that understanding is not synonymous with agreement. That simply understanding another's perspective does not imply that you agree with their perspective. They are two separate processes, yet understanding must precede agreement. You can't truly agree or disagree with something if you don't fully understand it.

There are three key practices that leaders demonstrate which show that they are effective listeners.

(a) asking others about their ideas and what they think
(b) being an active listener whose body language shows their interest
(c) listening patiently to different points of view

Many leaders are so full of enthusiasm that they find it difficult to be patient whilst others talk. Many because of their own expertise and experience interject solutions before the issue is fully explained. Breakthrough leaders exercise the discipline required to listen when they are genuinely trying to understand the other person. There are times of crisis, or when there is a need to make a decision quickly, that decisiveness, may be the appropriate response, but in developing others there is no substitute for taking the time to listen.

Anita Roddick, the transformational leader who built The Body Shop into a values-driven global retail empire, described the leadership style she looked for this way:

"For a leader to motivate and gain trust and loyalty a message via e-mail is not enough. Suggestion boxes are not enough either. Nor are employee surveys. Nor are graffiti facilities in the toilet. Nothing, but nothing, can substitute for a live leader listening and responding."

3. Acts on advice

A genuine act of empowerment is to show the other person the impact that they have and the extent to which they can influence outcomes. It is a demonstration of personal power and evidence of the difference I can make when I see how my ideas have been taken up and used productively.

The poor leader who wishes to make the other person feel ineffectual, simply ignores them and treats them as if they do not exist. The worst of leaders however are those who create a dependence which crushes initiative and results in blind obedience or unthinking compliance. This was characteristic of the "command and control" style of management exercised by autocratic leaders with their "my way or the highway" approach. These approaches were a good fit in bureaucratic organisations with their drive for consistency, standardisation and "no surprises", but in the world of today they are no longer appropriate.

The old style created dependency and in extreme cases what is termed in psychology as learned helplessness. This is a mental state where people feel that they have no control over their lives. We know that the fastest way to produce this mindset is to ask for advice and then ignore it. Consistently rejecting or ignoring people's suggestions, ideas and contributions is proven formula for inducing feelings of ineffectualness or helplessness.

On the other hand, we know that the best way to create an empowered person, is to show them how what they do has significance and to show them how their contributions and suggestions are taken seriously. Showing people how they can personally have an impact on results is an important step on the road to empowerment.

Asking for ideas and advice is a great way to create involvement, and taking on board ideas and advice is a great way to create ownership. It is ownership which produces discretionary effort where people do more than is expected and more than is required just to keep their job. If what you must do as part of your job is "required effort", then anything above and beyond that is "discretionary". It is discretionary in the sense that it is freely given, and can only be freely given by the person concerned. It can't be commanded or demanding, it's a voluntary act and we know that the more ownership a person feels for a job, the more it is freely given. This is the real hidden value in organisations and is the competitive advantage that transformational leaders are wanting to produce.

Many participants told stories about how they went beyond the call of duty repeatedly for breakthrough leaders who showed them how they could make a difference. Good managers and structured performance systems can get required behaviour. This is what you must do to keep your job. Setting stretch goals, tying them to key performance indicators and aligning rewards with outcomes are all effective ways to drive human behaviour. But none can guarantee to produce discretionary behaviour. This takes leadership and specifically leadership which works on a person's mindset and what we call the psychological contract. This is leadership which changes how people feel about their work and their commitments to it and how positively they feel about the future.

At the macro level this is achieved through cultures of empowerment and engagement. At the micro level it happens one to one when leaders see their job as developing talent and building the self-esteem personally of each individual.

There are three key practices that leaders exhibit here.

    (a) keeping an open mind and suspending judgement
    (b) empowering others to do the job
    (c) encouraging others to have their say

These are leaders who don't insist on having things done their way and give people the flexibility to bring their own personality to the way that they perform tasks. Leaders who only delegate keep the ownership and accountability with themselves. Leaders who empower their followers transfer ownership and accountability to the person performing the task. It is an essential part of the growth process that people be given greater ownership as their confidence and competence increase. Leaders who keep people dependent can never achieve breakthrough results and will never truly transform their organisations.

4. Sets a challenge and shows confidence in a person's ability to achieve it

The ability to set an appropriate challenge is the hallmark of an excellent motivator. It requires a great deal of insight into the psychological makeup of the person and a great deal of knowledge of the nature of the opportunity. Getting the right fit between potential and performance is quite an art. Too little stretch requires too little effort, too much stretch runs the risk of burning out, especially the precocious talent. In the past the prospective candidate for a challenging assignment could usually serve a key apprenticeship before moving into a position. Today talented people are required to step up "before" they are ready in many ways and then to use the stretch experience to accelerate their development.

This is a world where learning is the key asset and the test is the person's ability to learn faster than the rate of change. Most high performers love the rush that comes from being out of a comfort zone and thrive on the adrenalin of a steep learning curve. But the complexity is the degree of challenge. Too little and the thinking will be within the paradigm – it won't challenge the mindset enough. A degree of challenge is required whereby a person cannot address this issue with the current mode of thinking – otherwise they will typically resort to working harder or working longer. It needs a challenge whereby the person is forced to look at the issue anew and forced to challenge an existing mindset. The true steep learning curve is the ability to look at a problem or an opportunity with new eyes and with a new way of thinking.

Allied to challenging the thinking process is to challenge existing expectations. Setting a challenge should force a person to think beyond their current experience. It is intended to create some beginning dissatisfaction within the status quo. It is intended to break out of a prevailing complacency that many satisfactory performers exhibit.

This is the conundrum presented by Jim Collins in his classic book "From Good to Great", where he poses the question, is good really the enemy of great. His proposition is that many of us are good enough, achieving sufficient results, that we don't have the motivation to be great.

As Collins puts it in "From Good to Great":

"That good is the enemy of great is not just a business problem. It is a human problem. If we have cracked the code on the question of good to great, we should have something of value."

He continues that the key psychology of the journey from good to great is "to retain absolute faith that you can and will prevail in the end, regardless of the difficulties, and at the same time confront the most brutal facts of your current reality".

Breakthrough leaders not only set the challenge that will inspire, but also display absolute confidence in the person's ability to step up to the mark and to deliver at a higher level. Many respondents told stories of how their leaders were always looking for challenges and for opportunities to extend them and develop them further. They spoke of leaders who displayed overwhelming confidence in their ability and their capacity to deliver. They reported feeling a tremendous sense of responsibility and in some, sense of obligation. A feeling that they did not want to let their leader down. Some wanted to repay the faith shown in them, whilst others even though feeling some trepidation, also felt invigorated by the challenge.

There are three key practices for leaders who set challenges.

(a) seeking challenging assignments and opportunities
(b) showing confidence in others to achieve results
(c) setting stretch goals

These leaders take the view that their job is both to achieve results and to develop people. It is a poor leader who does not increase a follower's confidence and competence by some measure. Every year leaders and followers should be growing and developing. The test of the leader is to be able to say when moving on to the next job or assignment that, "I leave the people in better condition than they were when I arrived."

5. Coaches and provides support

Breakthrough leaders understand that challenging old ways of thinking and lifting people's aspirations and hopes, is only the start of the change process. Aspiration is the first step, realisation is the next step. The leader's challenge is to provide the support required as the follower ventures into new territory. In a way it is putting in place the safety net so that he/she can practice safely in an environment where both the psychological and physical risks have been minimised.

This is a critical part of the breakthrough process. It is a stage where many of us falter and retreat back to old ways of thinking and behaving. At the first sign of an impediment there is often a great temptation to retreat, because whilst the thought process is in place, we often have yet to develop the confidence to test ourselves fully.

It is like the golfer who understands the need to change his swing or the tennis player who appreciates the need to change his or her grip in order to improve their game. On big points, there is always the temptation to go back to the old way.

Unless one has the support to conquer self-doubt, it is often very difficult to persevere during adversity. This is where the coach has a crucial role to play. There is a crunch time and it is how it is mastered that will determine whether we move on or fall back to old ways of thinking. If we fall back, it takes even greater confidence and courage to try again. The leader needs to be attentive and supportive yet do so in a way which does not create dependency. It is not the coach's job to solve the problem. Their task is to help the follower to meet this challenge, to develop the resilience to stay the course and to embed new ways of behaving into new ways of thinking. The lessons derived from successfully meeting a challenge can alter one's self-belief and give one the confidence to tackle new and bigger challenges.

That coaching is a key skill for leaders was one of the most significant paradigm shifts in management thinking over the past twenty years. Trail blazers in this field were Tom Peters and Nancy Austin. In their classic book, "A Passion for Excellence" they argued that the leader's role as manager was helping people to overcome problems in performance and in the process assisting them to aspire to excellence.

They described leaders who are effective coaches as those who:

> Challenge people to do their best
> Care about how people are doing

Like to spend time with people
Listen exceptionally well
Keep promises
Make people confident

They made the point that leaders who are excellent coaches have high self-awareness and integrity and can build high trust relationships. It is in these high trust encounters that people can be open to express their doubts and fears and where the manager can gain greater insight into the degree of support that might be required to overcome the obstacles to change.

Breakthrough leaders accept that coaching is a major part of the support process. They understand that people will never change their thinking, just by doing things your way. They appreciate that people will not face the future with confidence unless they can deal with their fears and anxieties and learn how to ensure that they don't become impediments to development. In many workshops we heard participants talk about how their leaders had "supported me through some tough times"; "gave me the freedom to take a risk"; "encouraged me to try something new" and "gave me the courage to take on a new challenge" and "the confidence to believe I could succeed where others had not".

This is an important time in the process for testing new ideas and for challenging old ways of working. It's commonly referred to as moving out of your comfort zone. The reason why this is so hard is that by definition, a comfort zone is a place where one feels comfortable and has low levels of anxiety. Therefore, to move out of a comfort zone must be to move to a place of discomfort where you feel more anxious and insecure. It is not surprising that this is a place that most of us try to avoid. This is the test: if you are not feeling some level of discomfort, you are probably still in your comfort zone. The breakthrough leader must sense this and provide the coaching and support required to deal with discomfort, especially the psychological discomfort that arises from heightened anxiety.

There are three key practices that leaders who are excellent coaches display.

(a) putting in time to build specific skills and competence in others
(b) following through on promises made
(c) providing information and resources that others need to do their job

Breakthrough leaders deliberately target the development of skills so that followers can grow in confidence as their competence increases. Coaching and mentoring are the gifts that leaders give to their followers as they pass on knowledge and experience to a new generation of leaders. Support required is also situational and will vary according to the complexity of the task, the degree of challenge and the maturity of the follower.

6. Gives feedback and recognition

The final phase of the breakthrough process is giving feedback and recognition. It is through recognition and feedback that people feel that their efforts are appreciated and that their achievements are noted. It is how we begin to believe that our work has significance and that we can truly make a difference to our customers, our colleagues and our companies through what we do. Bringing meaning to work has been another of the key paradigm shifts that have occurred over the past twenty years in management thinking. In the past, work was regarded as a job, and a job was just a task one performed for pay. There was little consideration that work could be a source of fulfilment. Work was regarded as a burden, in fact, the burden of the working class.

The rise of knowledge workers globally has reduced the demand for manual labour and is now a major source of corporate value. McKinsey argue that a company must have an employee value proposition if they want to recruit and retain talent and that this must explain "why a smart, energetic, ambitious individual would want to come and work with you rather than with the team next door".

They continue that "creating a winning employee value proposition means tailoring a company's brand and products – the jobs it has to offer – to appeal to the specific people it wants to find and keep".

They raise the issue that feedback and coaching are an important part of the employee value proposition, because talented workers today want feedback on how they are performing and see it as a critical part of improving their performance, and thus in turn, making themselves more talented and more valuable.

The Gallup Organisation in their research into employee engagement and performance notes that companies pay a heavy price for disengaged workers because of their lower productivity. Their research demonstrates that the root cause of employee disengagement has consistently been poor management and two of the prime factors in this are the inability to set clear expectations and then to provide feedback.

Feedback is an important part of the breakthrough process. When it is skillfully given it can be instrumental in challenging existing modes of thinking and in sustaining commitment to a challenging change agenda. Associated with feedback is recognition. Everyone wants to feel appreciated and recognition is an important mechanism for expressing appreciation. James Kouzes and Barry Posner call this "encouraging the heart" and note that it is how leaders overtly link rewards with performance. They comment that "the climb to the top is arduous and long. People become exhausted, frustrated and disenchanted. They're often tempted to give up. Leaders encourage the heart of their constituents to carry on. It's part of the leader's job to show people how they can win."

Repeatedly in workshops participants spoke about the importance of feeling appreciated and how this helped to sustain and encourage them. They talked about leaders who "put the spotlight on me", "made me feel important in what I was doing", "gave me a profile in the company".

Breakthrough leaders use feedback and recognition to express appreciation to the people for their commitment and their work. It is a powerful mechanism for bringing meaning to work and for sustaining the flow of emotional energy required for significant change.

There are three key practices that distinguish leaders who are exceptional at providing feedback and recognition.

(a) acknowledging and putting the spotlight on the efforts of others
(b) celebrating success
(c) giving personal thanks

Breakthrough leaders know that recognition and appreciation are important mechanisms for sustaining effort especially during difficult times. Going out of our way, and finding the time to thank another for his or her contribution is a clear indicator of our care for others and a powerful demonstration of our concern. It is one of the simplest, yet most potent things that leaders do. One of the most courageous things that leaders do is to give direct candid feedback. This is very difficult for leaders who want to be loved and who don't want to confront the tough issues. Leaders who avoid difficult conversations do a disservice to the follower concerned.

These then are the distinctive characteristics of breakthrough leaders which differentiate them from leaders who, whilst they might be good managers, do not have the same transformational impact on their followers. The good news is that they are within the reach of all managers. The bad news is that they don't occur by accident. They are developed because managers see that they have a professional responsibility to develop the potential of their people and understand that the long-term success for their organisations will be determined by the extent to which that potential is brought out and then deployed.

Many managers don't develop these skills simply because they have a limited definition of their role. It is inevitable that as they see leadership becoming more central to what they do, the need to develop people will become more urgent.

The skills are developed by a process of deliberate practice. That is, managers get better at these behaviours, not just through development in general, but through development with specific focus and specific practice on each one. Practice makes perfect is correct. Managers get better at listening, by listening, and then by working on specific areas for improvement. The first step in this process is to bring the behaviours to awareness, and the second step is to have the discipline required for improvement. Ultimately managers need a framework which explains the interaction of factors which produce the breakthrough experience. This is very difficult for managers who have had very poor leadership models themselves. It will be much easier in the future as the practice of leadership improves and people in the workplace see more breakthrough leadership skills in action.

Chapter 7

The Attributes of Breakthrough Leaders

What breakthrough leaders stand for

What is extraordinary about the breakthrough leaders that were identified was not how exceptional they were, but in many ways how ordinary they were. As participants described the behaviours of leaders who had been so personally inspiring, what became apparent was how normal these behaviours were, and how much they were what people who care deeply about others do. They were not just what those in leadership positions do. Most of the behaviours described could also be applied to colleagues or team mates. In fact, in some companies where workshops were conducted, people struggled to think of any leaders who inspired them, but found it much easier to think of examples when the field was broadened out to include other people they had worked with in their careers who had inspired them.

Even in the case of identified leaders, few stood out in any way as being remarkable. In some cases the identified leaders were also in the workshop, in the same small group discussions, where they found themselves being discussed as the inspirational leader. Many did not fully comprehend the impact that they had had. They were aware of the results in terms of outcomes for the follower, but many had not fully appreciated the deep personal impact they had at the time on the person telling the story. In many cases they were pleased, but surprised, at the lasting impact and with the ease with which the followers were able to vividly recollect the situation. These leaders were able to put the exercise into perspective as they recalled the people who had in fact inspired them. It was in this situation that they, too, fully appreciated the impact of breakthrough leaders.

Teresa Amabile from Harvard Business School, found something similar in her research into leadership and creativity. She reported that "we often assume that leadership plays a central role in spurring creativity and innovation. But there is little empirical basis for this belief. The researchers were struck by the professional ways in which a manager's ordinary routine interactions with subordinates can support – or undermine creativity. We found that what these leaders said or did led team members to feel either more or less supported by the leader. That perceived level of leader support seemed to influence creative work down the road. Most of the successful leaders didn't by their own behaviours inspire creative ideas … they didn't present some lightning bolt idea … there was a process whereby seemingly trivial behaviours that leaders engaged in on a day to day basis would have a profound indirect influence."

Leaders who inspire come from all walks of life, at all stages in a career and at all levels in the organisation. What we found to be consistent was that they were accessible to their followers and able to challenge old ways of thinking and they did this by engaging in a set of behaviours.

As participants described breakthrough leaders, they also outlined certain attributes that go to the heart of the breakthrough interaction. In many ways they described what it was about their leader which inspired them. In this case it was the "who" of the leader as much as the "what" he or she did.

The attributes of the breakthrough leader that emerged were:

1. Treated others with respect
2. Built trust

3. Were optimistic
4. Team oriented
5. Clearly committed to learning
6. Deeply engaged
7. Personally involved
8. Passionate about a cause

Whether it is the context that influences the nature of the leaders and brings out these attributes, or it is the nature of the leader and their personal attributes which drive the context or situation is uncertain. It is not clear in which order they come, what it is more certain is that there is a dynamic interaction of attribute and context which delivers a truly remarkable result.

1. Breakthrough leaders treated others with respect.

These leaders showed a deep respect for others. They didn't tell them what to do although they certainly challenged. They didn't demand compliance although they were resolute in their belief in the other person. They showed respect primarily by taking the time, and through their body language they displayed what we call engaged listening. By this we mean listening that makes it obvious that one is involved. It's more than active listening, where one is attentive and receptive and perhaps uses what counsellors refer to as "minimal encouragers to talk". Engaged listening makes it obvious that you are there to share the journey with the other person. Questions that are asked have a twofold purpose. They are designed to create greater understanding and empathy on behalf of the questioner, but also intended to help the other person to think more clearly and to articulate more fully.

These leaders accept people as they find them and respect them for who they are. What they are concerned to uncover are impediments to the development of each person's potential, especially impediments which stem from a mindset which precludes each individual from seeking opportunities and challenges.

When people are in relationships of respect, they feel more valued and, as a consequence, more open in their communication. They are more open in two ways: more open with others and more open to others. That is, they are more candid in what they say and, in a reciprocal way, more open to be influenced by what others say.

2. Breakthrough leaders build trust.

It became apparent from the stories that we heard that the breakthrough leaders had the ability to build high levels of trust. This ability to build trust stems from two factors:

1. The leaders were rated high in personal integrity which was defined as keeping confidences, following through on commitments made, keeping promises and being honest in their dealings.
2. They were rated high on the absence of personal or hidden agendas. People felt they knew where they stood, they felt that the only agenda was their own development and not what was necessarily in the leader's best interests. In other words, these leaders would be prepared to put forward a person for promotion or let them move to another team in order to further their development, even if it left a gap in the leader's own team.

Trust in any organisation is critical for knowledge sharing and is at the heart of collaboration. Putting it simply, knowledge will never be shared above the level of trust that is established. In relationships where there is low trust, people are careful about what they disclose. When there is high trust, people will be more likely to admit errors and reveal mistakes.

High trust in a team leads to candid discussion and to frank feedback, but this is only productive where there is shared vision and a high degree of respect. High trust in a relationship builds confidence and leads both parties to be more open with each other. Leaders build trust because of who they are, as much as what they do. Breakthrough leaders build trust because their agendas are clear and because they make a genuine investment in the potential of their followers.

3. Breakthrough leaders are optimistic.

Breakthrough leaders are more optimistic in their assessments of the potential of their followers, and their capability to meet greater challenges. They were not always seen to be optimistic in regard to their own lives, but they certainly were when working with another's development. In other words, even those leaders who were more pessimistic by nature did not allow this to cloud their beliefs about the other's potential. They were able to bring a professional style to their work through their interactions and give the other person a greater sense of control of their own destiny. They do this by expanding their followers' options and choices and by building their belief in what is possible.

It is impossible to inspire someone through pessimism, through highlighting all the reasons why someone can't be successful. No coach can build self-belief in a team by concentrating on the impediments to victory and the hopelessness of the task. Irrespective of how he or she feels, a coach whilst being realistic about the obstacles, but must clearly be confident about the team's ability to succeed.

Martin Seligman, a leader in positive psychology, learned optimism and the debilitating effect of pessimism and learned helplessness, explains it this way:

"An optimistic explanatory style stops helplessness, whereas pessimistic explanatory style spreads helplessness. Your way of explaining events to yourself determines how helpless you become, or how energised, when you encounter everyday setbacks … what is crucial is what you think when you fail, using the power of "non-negative thinking". Changing the destructive things you say to yourself when you experience the setbacks that life deals all of us is the central skill of optimism."

An effective breakthrough leader helps people to put things into perspective, to challenge their negative self-talk and helps each individual to build a more optimistic and positive view about his or her future. They do this through their interactions, through their support and through their belief that each of us always has greater potential which can be developed and further challenges that can still be met.

4. Breakthrough leaders are team players.

These leaders believe in the power of the team. Even those who are more introverted by nature still believe in the collective power of the team and want to contribute in their own way to a greater team result. It's a matter of team spirit and the perspective that all individual efforts come together to build success. These leaders have the belief that each individual's work has significance and that when each person develops his or her potential, it has the power to lift the performance of the whole team.

This idea of connectedness also extends to the company vision and mission. These leaders have the belief that each individual's work contributes to the overall company strategy and that each person should set goals and aspirations that one to one lift the company towards its vision.

Sustaining commitment to any significant change process is also much easier in a team. A solo effort to change takes enormous reserves of willpower and self-discipline and can falter as the person tires or as stress builds up. Being a member of a cohesive team is a great source of strength. Teams can provide the passion and the energy which builds the resilience required to see change through. When one person stumbles the others can provide support, when one person has a bad day the others can quickly put it into a bigger perspective.

High performance teams access the full diversity of skills found in any group of people. The best lift the achievement threshold for all members and because they can invariably perform better than any group of individuals they can be a great source of pride. The diversity of skills and the performance focus means that they can provide the environment for innovation and original thought which enriches not only the team and the company but each individual member as well.

5. Breakthrough leaders are committed to learning.

These leaders have a passion for learning, for finding a better way, for challenging the status quo. They were often described as curious with an insatiable desire to learn. Command and control managers placed less emphasis on learning but in a world of disruptive technologies and rapid change the need to build greater capability faster and with greater agility is paramount.

Leaders need to break through resistance to change. This not only becomes a competitive necessity, but also a personal survival priority. As the nature of the competition changes and boosts in individual and team performance are demanded, those who cannot respond will be left behind. Every time there is a shift in competitive strategy and every time new technology disrupts established capabilities, there is a resultant sea-change in skills, attitudes and responsibilities required by large sections of the workforce. The ability to change, to learn and to adapt is basic to long-term employment.

Leaders at the personal level play a huge role in creating a context for change and a climate for learning. Legendary business leader, Jack Welch, was an early advocate for leaders to be learners and challenged them to build learning organisations. He pointed out that "the biggest competitive advantage that a company can have is creating an environment where people can learn from each other. You have to have an insatiable desire to learn."

6. Breakthrough leaders are deeply engaged.

It is not breath-taking oratory that is called for, or the charm of the charismatic leader that is needed, but the sincerity of the leader with a deep commitment to the development of others. These things undoubtedly have impact but it is an impact that soon fades if not followed up. It soon fades because the excitement of the moment is quickly replaced by the harsh light of reality once a doubting mindset gets to work. No matter how excited a person gets, if in their heart of hearts they don't believe they can do it, then motivation soon fades.

Sporting coaches soon realise that motivational talks have little effect in the context of the game. It's the game plan, the skills training, the specific challenge on the field that is important and enduring. Rather than "revving players up", most coaches are trying to calm them down so they can concentrate on the task at hand. It's about harnessing emotion and expressing it intelligently and about countering negative thought patterns. A good coach knows how to blend the right amount of challenge and support.

In a business context it is similar. The highly effective leader can blend the right amount of I.Q. and E.Q. (emotional intelligence). The I.Q. is about logic, about making the business case, about explaining what it is that the person needs to do. The E.Q. is about being in touch with the person's emotional reaction, understanding their motivational drivers and appreciating the personal dimension of each challenge set. The breakthrough leader blends I.Q. and E.Q. in presenting the opportunity as well as recognising fears and anxieties, and can work in both the cognitive and affective domains. Sometimes the challenge requires more logic, sometimes more empathy. Sometimes the person requires more convincing and other times more understanding.

The experienced breakthrough leader is deeply engaged with the mindset of the follower and uses a repertoire of interactive approaches, each one with a specific style, each one to serve a specific purpose and each one to address the mindset of the follower concerned. The styles range from simply creating awareness through to building learning capability.

Awareness. The leader wanting to create awareness simply restricts the interaction at this stage, to informing, to highlighting issues, to bringing things to another's attention.

Understanding. The leader wanting to build understanding will use a more interactive exchange where there is room for questions and answers from all parties involved.

Agreement. The leader wanting to formulate an agreement will listen to all perspectives, engage in greater discussion and will seek to develop a shared explanatory framework.

Commitment. The leader wanting to secure commitment will draw others into building the case for change, encourage their contribution and open pathways to give them ownership of the change process.

Disciplined action. The leader wanting to take action understands that to turn commitment into a disciplined plan of action, requires clear expectations, relevant resources, appropriate skills and common criteria for success.

Learning. The leader wanting to promote learning will assume the role of a mentor or facilitator and rely more on the power of review and reflection as the catalysts for learning and change.

7. Breakthrough leaders are personally involved.

The major complaint about most leaders is that they are neither visible nor accessible. Leaders are always busy with many competing demands for their time, but their impact is limited unless people see them and can spend time with them.

Leaders have three constituent groups in their immediate sphere of influence that they need to be personally involved with. They have their boss, their peer group and their direct reports. If they wish to influence the business agenda or the strategic direction of their company, they need to be able to manage up. If they wish to build a collaborative culture they need to influence in a more collegial sense. Both of these groups require some time and some strategic thought. However, it is the last of the three, the direct reports, who need the greatest personal involvement. The success of the company in large part is driven more down the line than up the line. The cascading effect is a real multiplier effect and bringing the vision, culture and strategy to the front line is where it is ultimately and directly brought to life.

It is breakthrough leaders at all levels who are the architects of this process. It is these leaders who unlock potential one at a time, situation by situation. It is not a one size fits all approach, it is deeply personal and demands considerable involvement between the leader and each individual.

Marcus Buckingham and Curt Coffman from the Gallup Organisation put it well when they write that:

"Companies are searching for undiscovered reserves of value. Human nature is one of those last, vast reserves of value. If they are to increase their value, companies know that they must tap these reserves. You, the manager, are the best mechanism they have."

In other words, the challenge for leaders is primarily psychological. It is more interpersonal than operational. It is for astute leaders to find the best mechanisms for bringing out the best in individuals. It is an individual task, one to one, and very personal, to find out how to make each person more fulfilled, more effective and further developed than they were before.

8. Breakthrough leaders have a passion for a cause.

The best leaders are passionate about what they do. For them it is more than a job, it is a chance to achieve something worthwhile. They are motivated by the desire to make a difference, to make a mark, to leave an imprint. They look for the opportunity to go beyond just what is required to complete the task. They bring a considerable discretionary effort to their work, beyond simple motivation and beyond just enthusiasm. They have a deep sense of engagement with what they do and are driven by a strong sense of purpose which brings great clarity to the choices they make on a daily basis.

This deep motivation is something that Daniel Goleman identified as the hallmark of the new leadership style.

"If there is one trait that virtually all effective leaders have, it is motivation. They are driven to and achieve beyond expectations – their own and everyone else's. Plenty of people are motivated by external factors such as a big salary. By contrast those with leadership potential are motivated by a deeply embedded desire to achieve for the sake of achievements. The first sign is a passion for the work itself."

It is hard to inspire others if you are bored and frustrated. In short, it is hard to inspire others if you are not inspired yourself. It is certainly impossible if you are bitter, resentful and cynical. Leaders with negative emotions such as these certainly have an impact on the people they lead, but it is a dampening effect. They suck the life out of enthusiasm and take the drive out of ambition. Leaders who are cynical have given up trying and they have shut down on learning. Cynicism is the direct enemy of learning, because once you are cynical you believe there is no point in learning and in trying to change things for the better.

Such leaders have a contagious effect and can quickly kill all hope of improvement. In a similar way, leaders with positive emotions are equally infectious. They spread enthusiasm and hope. They create climates of opportunity and innovation. They do this best when they are working for a cause in which they truly believe.

We can probably all recall teachers through our school years who were passionate about the subjects they taught. Many of the stories that participants recounted about inspirational leaders, were stories about these teachers. They recalled the energy they created through their passion and about the lasting motivational effect this passion had on the lives of their students.

Daniel Goleman and his team have been researching what they call resonant leadership, which is the ability these leaders have to deeply touch their followers and to motivate them in a profound way.

They write:

> "These leaders articulate where a group is going, but not how it will get there and setting people free to innovate, experiment and take calculated risks. Knowing the big picture and how a given job fits in gives people clarity. Visionary leaders help people to see how their work fits into the big picture, and give people a sense that what they do matters. This maximises buy in for the organisation's overall long-term goals and strategy."

An important part of the transformational process is the energy these leaders bring. They can literally change the lives of their followers by connecting them to a larger cause and by showing them how, through their work, they are making a difference to the lives of others. People will bring considerably more discretionary effort to a cause than to a job. To this end it is the ability of leaders to describe their organisation's vision and mission in inspiring terms that brings a daily sense of purpose to the work of their teams.

There is no doubt that the breakthrough leaders in this research are excellent leaders. They are excellent because of the impact they had, not because they are exceptional human beings. It is the combination of attributes and behaviours which produces the result. Whilst the behaviours can be learnt by deliberate practice, the attributes are more intrinsically tied up with the character and values of the leader.

Having said that, a sophisticated leadership style can be nurtured and developed and cultivated and can become a leadership strength. Treating others with respect and building trust are leadership attributes. Being optimistic and having a commitment to learning are also assets to leadership. Being a team player, deeply engaged, personally involved and passionate about a cause are also key attributes explored in this research. It is probable that without these attributes at least to some degree one would struggle to be a leader. It is the extent to which these are identified, nurtured and developed that may define the success of the breakthrough leader.

Chapter 8

The Breakthrough Process

Changing mindsets in action

The essential purpose of the breakthrough process is to change the mindset. That is to change how people think about themselves, about their potential and about their capacity to make a greater contribution to results and outcomes. Although much of the theory in this area is in the realm of psychology, and especially cognitive psychology, it has also attracted the attention of researchers from education and other allied fields.

Edward De Bono, the originator of the term lateral thinking, has advocated for a range of approaches to teach flexibility in thinking. His most popular one has been his Six Thinking Hats. This is a framework which suggests the utilisation of six distinct thinking perspectives as a problem solving technique. De Bono maintains that people can be trained to see the world from a new perspective if they adopt a disciplined approach to the way that they think.

De Bono believes that techniques like these can be adopted by people irrespective of their psychology, their self-esteem and their level of intelligence. He believes that all people can be taught and trained to think more clearly. He is not concerned with mindset change, simply with applying cognitive skills, to produce more creative and effective thinking. De Bono's approach has achieved widespread appeal and his methods have been applied globally and have been credited with helping many people and organisations to be more disciplined in their thinking and decision-making processes. But they are not intended or designed to deal with issues of mindset change. Their concern is the development of thinking skills not with psychological processes within the individual. They are not a pathway to self-awareness and self development. This is a challenge which looks more for its answers to psychology.

Mindset Change

Howard Gardner, Professor of Education at Harvard University, has devoted his professional life to exploring how people think, the nature of intelligence and changing mindsets. In "Changing Mindsets", Gardner describes what he calls the art and science of changing our own and other people's minds.

He explains that the challenge is less about new ways of thinking and more about the reluctance to let go of old ways of thinking. He writes that "if I could dispense just one morsel of advice to mind changers, it is to spend less time trying to convince individuals of a new perspective, and more time trying to understand and thereby to neutralise the resistance".

It is a principle of game theory that people are more concerned about avoiding a loss than they are motivated to make a gain. He concludes that getting people to let go of the old cannot be done without a high degree of trust. He explains that, "when one trusts a person one feels at ease, one resonates with that entity. By the same token a loss of trust signals a diminution or disappearance of resonance, and a correlative rise in resistance. Much of one's capacity to change the minds of others hinges on whether or not one is trusted, seen as trustworthy".

This corresponds with the research presented in Chapter Four which found that breakthrough leaders build trust, and this trust then provides the foundation for the inspiring and supportive practices which follow.

Gardner cautions that it is very hard to change how people think and yet that is central to work of managers and leaders. Changing how people think about a new strategy, changing how people think about collaborating across functional areas, changing how people think about their own potential and the contribution they might make are all basic examples of daily life in organisations. Gardner believes that leaders are by definition "people who change minds", but warns that this cannot be done in a way that is deceptive, manipulative or by compulsion.

He believes that if trust is to be maintained, mindset change must be done in a transparent way, an open way, a learning way. It must be done on the basis of informed consent, and a willingness to embrace a new way of seeing things. In the end the forces of change must be greater than the power of the resistance for mindset change processes to be truly effective. The leader's role is to find the most effective way to help people to let go of the past and to embrace the new.

As Geoffrey Colvin writing in Fortune Magazine noted when commenting on the turbulence and uncertainties facing organisations today:

> "Managing amid chaos has become the central problem for companies of every kind. It is a predicament that arises from the very nature of today's economy. And the solution requires a retraining not of skills but of mindset and assumptions. The biggest challenge has less to do with corporate strategy or management structures than with the nature of human beings and our instinctive reactions to change.

The challenge is getting comfortable with it – especially hard because modern corporations were created explicitly to resist chaos. If we're in a truly revolutionary business age, it would be crazy to think that more radical change isn't coming. The challenge: finding the will to embrace it."

Many of the mindsets that were considered to be an asset in the past are seen as a liability today. Changing these mindsets is a key challenge for leaders and for humanity itself in an age where machines are assuming an increasingly central role.

Learned Optimism

Another approach that sheds light on this challenge is that put forward by Martin Seligman, who is a past president of the American Psychological Society. Seligman is a pioneer of the positive psychology movement, which is a new field of psychology that looks at human development from a growth and optimistic perspective, rather than a sickness and pessimistic perspective. Seligman's trailblazing research was to discover the origins of optimism and pessimism and to gain greater insight into the concepts of learned helplessness and resilience.

Seligman proposed that it was less of what happened to people in their life and more their interpretations of these events that had the greatest impact on their thinking and their subsequent behaviour. It wasn't so much whether an event was good or bad or had a positive or negative impact that had the dominant effect, but whether or not the individual interpreted the event as positive or negative. It wasn't the event itself but thinking about the event that was the key.

According to Seligman, people develop a sense of "learned helplessness" and underachieve, not because of what life does to them but because of how they think about their life. A great deal of this thinking can be described as self-limiting thinking because it is, in effect, a self-fulfilling prophecy. This occurs when the greatest impediment to a person's development is their own thinking and not a lack of opportunity available to them.

The breakthrough process is intended to help a person make the shift from a self-limiting mindset to a breakthrough mindset.

Two mindsets at work

Self limiting	Breakthrough
• Pessimistic	• Optimistic
• Reactive	• Proactive
• Problem centered	• Opportunity seeking
• Closed	• Open
• Doubting	• Confident
• Compliant	• Empowered
• Disengaged	• Engaged
• Cautious	• Courageous

Making the shift from a self limiting to a breakthrough mindset

What causes a person to be in many ways their own worst enemy? Part of the answer lies in patterns of thinking they have established, which are often ingrained from early childhood experience. It may have stemmed from an inability to deal with past failure or disappointment. It will almost certainly be associated with low self-esteem or a lack of confidence.

Martin Seligman "Learned Optimism", describes the precursor as a pessimistic rather than an optimistic outlook. He suggests that everyone inside of them has a "yes" or a "no" deeply embedded in their thinking and that this word was implanted in response to early childhood experience. According to Seligman it was less the nature of the experience and more how the person made sense of life's adversity which framed this predisposition.

According to Seligman "the defining characteristic of pessimists is that they tend to believe that bad events will last a long time and will undermine everything that they do. The optimists confronted by adversity think about it in the opposite way. These two habits of thinking about causes have consequences. Literally hundreds of studies show that pessimists give up more easily and that optimists do much better. I have found however that pessimism is escapable. Pessimists can learn to be optimists".

Seligman constructed a theory and a methodology for overcoming the debilitating effects of pessimism and to learning to develop an optimistic outlook. He established that it wasn't the event itself which coloured the thinking, but rather the explanatory style. It was how a person interpreted the event rather than the event itself which was the issue. Some develop a pessimistic explanatory style whilst others develop a positive explanatory style. The pessimistic style we know can be debilitating and can reduce motivation and hope. It becomes a core ingredient of a self-limiting mindset. Whereas the optimistic style is positive and encouraging and becomes the lynch pin of a breakthrough mindset.

What this means is that to deal effectively with a pessimistic explanatory style the negative think needs to be surfaced and challenged.

The first step is to bring negative self-thought to the surface. The second step is to expose it for what it is. The third step is to see that it is essentially self -defeating. The fourth step is to have the courage to challenge it by taking action. All of this needs a supportive leader or someone who has a genuine belief in the potential of the person and can identify opportunities that might be available. It is a genuine interest in the worth and development of others that the breakthrough leader brings to this process.

Seligman discovered that people can overcome a negative perspective, not by motivational gimmicks, or by the power of positive thinking, but by changing the way they think. Seligman writes: "we have found over the years that positive statements you make to yourself have little if any effect. What is crucial is what you think."

In reality this means that the impact of the charismatic leader will always be mediated by the explanatory style of the follower. The enthusiasm and inspiration generated by charisma will soon subside in mind of the pessimist. On the other hand, it can be sustained and harnessed as a source of strength in the mind of the optimist.

To make matters worse, the pessimist can quickly turn the success of the charismatic leader into an additional source of dissatisfaction as it can be perceived as highlighting the difference between leader and follower and in this way can be used to reinforce the negative image of the follower in comparison with the leader.

It is not the leader's personal example which produces the result, but the nature and quality of the interaction which enables the follower to challenge self -limiting and, ultimately, self -defeating thinking.

The Breakthrough Process

In a very practical and applied way Martyn Newman, a consulting psychologist and specialist in emotional intelligence, describes the breakthrough process when he writes:

"The good news is that although your explanatory style over time has become a habit, you can learn to change this mindset. How you interpret an event is under your control ... you can learn to think and succeed like an optimist by changing your explanatory style, even if you are a confirmed pessimist."

The breakthrough process can be stimulated by the charismatic leader, but it takes more than charisma to sustain it. The complete process requires a leader who can take the time to understand the person, to build confidence, and to give the support needed to challenge and to confront self imposed limitations. It takes courage to step outside of a comfort zone and to venture into unknown or at least unfamiliar territory. To take the first step requires someone who can see the opportunity. To sustain the journey requires the helping hand of the supportive leader. The breakthrough leader provides the safety net which enables the doubtful person to take the first step and then to keep on moving. This does not happen in an instant, but is a journey which has to be sustained with daily initiatives over a period of time.

Whilst breakthrough leaders are primarily concerned with personal development, they always have to consider this development within the context of the organisation and its strategy, culture and vision. In this way they align the personal process with the transformational change that the organisation, business unit or team is undertaking. In brief there are at least four stages that organisations pass through in most transformational change processes.

The stages are:-

1. Engagement
2. Involvement
3. Empowerment
4. Inspiration

The first stage is where the leader engages the follower in the vision. Creating shared vision is a powerful means by which people can be inspired to pursue a common cause. The vision speaks to something within the person, whereby each individual comes to believe that he or she can contribute, and even more would like to contribute, to the achievement of the vision. During this stage, the vision is discussed and the challenge explained.

Once the individual is engaged with the vision, the next step is to make it personally meaningful. This stage is one of involvement where each individual can see the contribution he or she can make in practical, applied terms. This requires more of an exchange between leader and follower and means that the individual must be able to see the significance of what they do for the final result. It is during this stage that commitment is established and embedded and becomes the foundation for the accountability requirements that follow.

The next stage is to empower each person given that they have the ability and resources to make a contribution. During this stage specific objectives and priorities are established and accountabilities defined. The empowerment stage is critical especially in knowledge based organisations where people work autonomously and are given the ownership for the task, the process and the outcomes. It is also required in globally dispersed organisations and in virtual teams where individuals are working remotely from head office. The empowerment stage is concerned with giving the person ownership and accountability for the task or process. Through ownership people accept a profound sense of responsibility for action taken and outcomes achieved.

The final stage is to sustain the effort. The leader's task is one of renewal and inspiration in order to keep people energised and inspired over the long haul. It is during this stage that the leader is building the resilience of the team to be able to cope with adversity and set-backs. The loop is completed and the process begins again as the leader continues to constantly refresh the vision and monitors that each individual is still engaged.

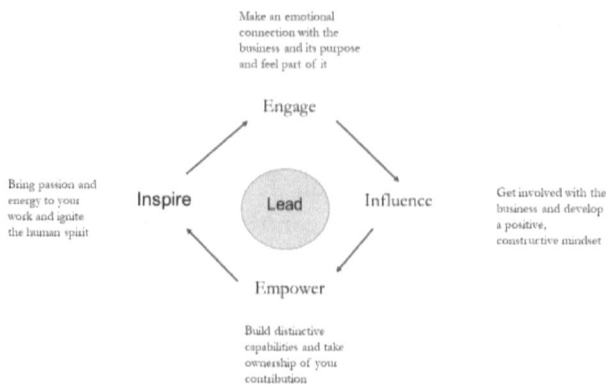

The process of transformational change

During these stages, the process is sustained, the relationship is deepened and the transformation is nurtured by the six distinctive breakthrough behaviours. During the change process, the leader is also employing the breakthrough behaviours as a daily style of leading. For example, showing a genuine interest in the worth and development of others is not just for the engagement stage, although engagement won't proceed without it. It is a behaviour that must be part of the leader's repertoire during all stages. It is fundamental to establishing a supportive yet challenging environment and it is the basis upon which leaders are able to bring out the best in others.

Whilst we can see how the leader behaves to stimulate and sustain the breakthrough process, the impact on the individual concerned is also quite clear. Self-limiting thinking and the inability to achieve your potential is essentially a de-motivating experience. Most people start life with the drive to grow and develop. A child cannot stop learning, stop exploring the world and cannot stop the gradual unfolding of their own unique potential.

Over time in many organisations, a person becomes reconciled to living a life less fulfilled. Gradually cynicism develops to mask the gap between what is and what might have been. The creeping pull of cynicism can be seen clearly in the young recruit who joins an organisation full of hope and vision, only to become "bitter and twisted" in the face of missed opportunities and serial disappointment. Often these people have a career which has stalled or plateaued, and some would be described as being in a comfort zone.

It takes quite an exceptional and supportive leader to reawaken aspirations and to re-energise and re-motivate this group. This challenge is not restricted to the older workforce, it can also be present in new recruits who have low aspirations based on limited expectations of their own potential. Many organisations have a culture of complacency with little focus on growth and development. This rapidly changes when they recognise the strategic asset that lies within their grasp if they can release the potential of their entire workforce.

Organisations are only too well aware of the difficulty of kick-starting the growth process and the challenge of dealing with what is often deeply ingrained habitual behaviour. In many companies, early enthusiasm in a career has given way to disappointment and deep cynicism. Some of this can be attributed to a lack of ambition by being in the wrong job, but more can be attributed to poor leadership. Organisations are continuing to bear the consequences of poor recruiting and mediocre management to this day. A legacy has been left in the mind of much of the workforce that has resulted in low expectations, low engagement and low performance. It is a significant challenge to turn this around.

Four Keys to Unlock Breakthrough

Competent, concerned managers can initiate the breakthrough process but can only sustain it as they unlock four key qualities in the individuals concerned. These are:-

1. Confidence
2. Capability
3. Courage
4. Conviction

Breakthrough leaders seek to build the confidence of people, and frequently rebuild that confidence if it has been undermined. They seek to build greater confidence in each person's ability to contribute and to perform and to do more than they are currently doing. They do this by making people feel valued and important, seeking opportunities and challenges for them and by engaging and involving them in decision-making processes of the organisation.

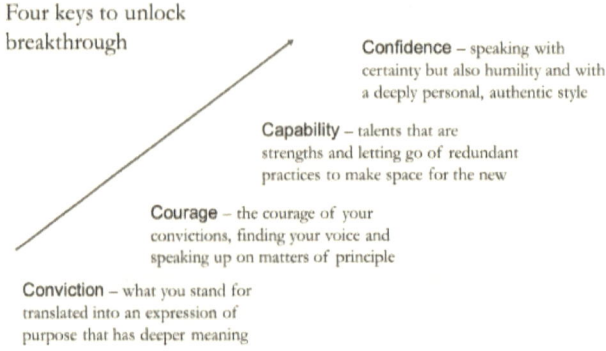

Four keys to unlock breakthrough

Confidence – speaking with certainty but also humility and with a deeply personal, authentic style

Capability – talents that are strengths and letting go of redundant practices to make space for the new

Courage – the courage of your convictions, finding your voice and speaking up on matters of principle

Conviction – what you stand for translated into an expression of purpose that has deeper meaning

At the same time, they seek to develop and build individual capability in line with the challenges offered. This is done through coaching and mentoring, but often on the job through challenging assignments and projects and sometimes through formal skills development programs. Supportive performance management systems can also play an important role here.

As the confidence and capability increase, there is a need to have the courage to meet the challenge, accept uncertainty and to move out of one's "comfort zone". Breakthrough leaders do this through the support they offer and the feedback they provide. It takes courage to leave the security of habitual ways of doing things and as we have seen, "leaving the old" is usually a greater source of anxiety than "embracing the new".

What places these three in context and provides the required focus for change is a conviction, or deep belief in the worth of the cause and a personal commitment to one's own contribution. Breakthrough leaders help their people to explore their own needs and motivations and help them to bring the organisation's vision and purpose to life. They understand that conviction can only deepen when there is a close alignment between individual wants and organisational needs. Clearly articulating organisational vision and values and making these personally relevant for each individual is in many ways the central driving force of breakthrough leadership.

This research shows that leaders when they use breakthrough behaviours are likely to have an emotional and psychological impact on their followers. This is then applied as a leadership style throughout the four stages of the transformational change process. In this way when leaders consistently and genuinely adopt breakthrough behaviours they produce certain key qualities in their followers which enable them not only to be more effective personally, but also to make a greater contribution to the success of the organization.

These elements of breakthrough leadership were clearly articulated by Sir Terry Leahy, who was C.E.O. of Tesco, and the architect of the group's period of dramatic global growth. Reflecting on his time at Tesco he commented.

"I think that working in Tesco and working with people has taught me that the important thing is what you cause other people to do rather that what you do yourself. And so over time you learn that it's much more about motivating and inspiring other people and challenging other people to do more. So in your leaders you want confidence, somebody who you want to listen to and somebody who makes you feel good about yourself and about your capability and gives you the courage and the optimism to take on a challenge and succeed.

I believe a lot in people. I believe a lot in the potential of people. I have never lost that belief that people are capable of incredible things if you give them the confidence and the opportunity".

Similarly, James McNerney, who was C.E.O. of Boeing expressed a similar view:

"I start with people's growth, my own growth included. I don't start with the company's strategy or products. I start with people's growth because I believe that if the people who are running and participating in a company grow, the company's growth will in many respects take care of itself. I have this idea in my mind all of us get 15% better every year. Usually that means your ability to lead, to chart the course for your employees, to inspire them to reach for performance and to have the courage to do the right thing.

I tend to think of this in terms of helping others get better. I view myself as a value-added facilitator here. What I do is figure out how to unlock that [potential] in people, because most people have that inside them. But they get trapped in a bureaucratic environment where they've been beaten about the head and shoulders."

THE BREAKTHROUGH OUTCOMES			
Outcome	Too Much	Balance	Too Little
1. Confidence	Complacency Arrogance	Humility	Doubt Caution
2. Capability	Inflexibility Non Adaptable	Curiosity	Inadequacy Insecurity
3. Courage	Non Strategic Compulsive	The four qualities need to be in balance as an over emphasis on Discretion	Fear Anxiety
4. Conviction	Zealous Close Minded	Compassion	Apathy Boredom

Breakthrough Outcomes

The four qualities need to be in balance as an over emphasis on one alone can have unintended consequences and prevent a person from making their optimum contribution and from fulfilling his or her potential.

Not all people in the workplace, for example, need greater confidence. There are some who have more confidence than their performance warrants and some have higher expectations than their contributions deserve. An over reliance on confidence can lead to arrogance or complacency and an unfounded belief in one's ability to meet challenges without the need for outside support. Confidence needs to be balanced with the humility that one does not have all the answers and still has much to learn. It is a confidence born out of a realistic assessment of one's own strengths and potential that is required. It is self-confidence not self-delusion which is the cornerstone of the breakthrough experience.

Too great a belief in one's own capability can lead to inflexibility and reluctance to work outside of an area of specialist expertise or function. Being the expert can reinforce habitual modes of operating and produce an unwillingness to collaborate with others with different capabilities and strengths. Confidence in one's own capability needs to be balanced with a curiosity to learn more and to see things from different perspectives. The drive for flexibility which is a strategic necessity for most organisations today requires workers who are highly adaptable, and who also have a clear aptitude for learning. The demands of growth mean that many workers are put into jobs which are clearly a stretch for them and are placed into positions where in the past they may have been considered not fully ready. Being able to handle a steep learning curve is today a career asset and breakthrough leaders give their followers the support and coaching which enable them to succeed.

Too much personal courage can lead a person to take unwarranted risks and to confront challenges head on rather than in a more strategic fashion. The ability to see the bigger strategic picture and to take the time to reflect before acting can be sacrificed because of unrestrained impulsivity and a keen determination to succeed. Courage needs to be tempered by discretion and the ability to be able to consider more than one course of action and to resist the impulse to "just do it". Highly charismatic leaders can often motivate their followers to a course of action which with hindsight might well be regarded as ill-conceived or inadequately considered. Breakthrough leaders are concerned to give their followers the personal courage to move more easily out of what might be a comfort zone and to accept greater personal and professional challenge.

Conviction is the quality which brings purpose to the other three. However, used to extremes or exclusively, it can lead to single mindedness and intolerance of other perspectives. Group-think is often a consequence of the over zealous pursuit of what seems to all concerned to be a worthwhile purpose. Conviction needs to be balanced by the compassion that assumes good intent in others and accepts the legitimacy of opposing points of view. Without the conviction that the challenge is worthwhile few people would strive to change. The breakthrough leader must know each follower well enough to know something of their individual dreams and aspirations, even if the follower concerned finds this difficult to articulate.

Developing people and helping them to overcome self-limiting thinking is not a one time challenge. It is not something a leader does once and which produces a transformational change. It has to become a daily part of the breakthrough leader's repertoire. It is through consistent disciplined action that these leaders achieve breakthrough results and produce sustainable change in the person concerned.

It is through the breakthrough process that leaders imbue their followers with the confidence, the capability and the courage to meet the challenges they face and to do this with the conviction to ensure that development has a deeper purpose and that the unfolding of potential has a truly worthwhile aim.

Chapter 9

The Nature of Inspiration

Building an inspired workplace

It is clear that how we think about leadership continues to change. The Center for Creative Leadership in North Carolina, has established a world class reputation for developing leadership capability, where relationships have a central focus. This is major shift from leadership as a role or positional construct to where leadership is a capability of all humans.

Paradoxically, this shift is not evident in practice to large segments of the working population. It may be that leaders think it is happening but its impact is not yet being felt in the workforce generally. It has been widely reported over many years that only half of the U.S. workers were happy with their jobs and only fourteen percent were very satisfied. Business Week observed that when people are uninspired at work, it shows in their behaviour and their commitment.

The Workplace is Still a Sad Reality for Many

However, this is not just an issue for the United States, it is in reality a global issue. In Australia studies looking at employee satisfaction and motivation have found that the quality of management is the big issue: it is the number one factor of importance in looking for a job and the number one source of dissatisfaction when in the job.

Over time surveys have consistently revealed that the majority of workers:

> are unhappy with their work
> are very dissatisfied with the quality of management
> think their managers aren't open and honest
> think that their managers don't listen
> think their managers don't inspire trust
> say their managers don't provide regular feedback
> say their managers don't respond to suggestions

A pretty dismal picture of what would appear to be the prevailing climate in many Australian workplaces. In fact, you could easily conclude that the majority of Australian workplaces have a long way to go simply to put in place effective management practices that can develop people and improve their performance. The good news however, is that most management issues are easily addressed because it is simple actions (eg. setting clear expectations, giving feedback, appreciation), not necessarily sophisticated communication skills that have the greatest positive impact on employee's attitudes to work. It may be that many managers do not have the knowledge or the basic skills to effectively manage and it may be ignorance and lack of development and training opportunities that is the basic problem.

Taking this into account, it is still reasonable to ask why it is that workers in such large numbers are not inspired in their work? Most of the evidence points to the nature of the relationship with their manager. It may be as much what managers don't do as what they do that is the problem. If, as it seems, many managers don't know how to inspire, perhaps even how to lead, they certainly can't be expected to know how to change mindsets.

Inspiration in the Workplace

Carmine Gallo writes in "Ten Simple Secrets of the World's Greatest Communicators", that "the secret to inspiring is to paint a picture of a world made better by your service, product, company or cause". He goes on to express sympathy for workers who come to work fired up to do a great job, "only to be deflated by their uninspiring supervisors".

It may be that being attracted by the great vision is the source of inspiration, but it is also true that this may be a very transient experience if it is not supported by the on-going relationship with your manager. The managers who participated in this research reported in this book were able to recall times when they were profoundly inspired to achieve, and they were able to recall also that it was the relationship with their leaders which gave them the self-belief to overcome doubt and the courage to confront the unknown. They were able to give example after example of leaders who built confidence, who could see their potential and who gave them the courage to step out of their comfort zone. There were also countless stories of leaders who blocked inspiration, who undermined confidence and who sapped energy. In essence, breakthrough leaders mobilise inspiration. They mobilise inspiration to connect people to the larger purpose in their work and they also use inspiration to give people the passion and energy required for change.

But what does it mean to be inspired at work? To be inspired at work is to be energised and filled with the belief that what I do is worthwhile, and with the self assurance that I am capable of contributing to a greater purpose. There are two aspects to the process. One is that the organisation has some worthwhile purpose, and second is the belief that what I do through my work directly contributes to that purpose. It is very difficult for leaders to inspire others if they are not inspired themselves. When they are inspired, leaders are passionate to engage their followers and their passion is infectious. Work can easily become just another job without a compelling purpose which brings meaning to it. It is for leaders to look first within themselves to find the meaning for which they work, and to identify the source of fulfilment in their own lives. As we know not all work is exciting and fulfilling, but leaders need to keep the bigger picture in mind so that they can maintain the passion that they need to inspire others.

At every level of seniority in an organisation every person wants to feel that what they do has significance. Making a difference is a fundamental human motivation. It is not just that I am aligned with a vision that makes a difference, but that I make a difference to that vision through the work that I do. Daniel Goleman calls this being attuned and describes it as "leaders being in touch with their own thoughts and feelings and communicating to followers in a way which touches their hearts". Attunement is a level of emotional engagement beyond that required for alignment and gives people the confidence and self-belief to feel that they can make a contribution.

Attunement is not simply an intellectual partnership where people are aligned through common interests. It is beyond being aligned through having similar attitudes. It is different from both of these and is a level of engagement where people connect at a deeper level and is built on trust, respect, and a belief in each person's worth, potential and contribution. It is when leaders can connect with their followers at this deeper level that the relationship can lay the foundations for inspiration.

Inspiration is defined by the Oxford Dictionary as "the breathing in of some ideas or purpose into the mind". The Indian philosopher, Patanjali, was more expansive in arguing more than two thousand years ago that the inspirational and breakthrough processes are essentially exercises in lifting the self-esteem of people. He writes:

"When you work for yourself, or for your own personal gain, your mind will seldom rise above the limitations of an undeveloped life. But when you are inspired by some great purpose, some extraordinary project, all your thoughts break your bonds: your mind transcends limitations, your consciousness expands in every direction, and you find yourself in a new, great and wonderful world. Dormant forces, faculties and talents become alive, and you discover yourself to be a greater person by far than you ever dreamed yourself to be."

A Case-study: Inspiration in action in Bunnings Warehouse

Finding ways to inspire their leaders so that they in turn can inspire their people and their teams, has been a key ingredient in the success of many companies. In Australia, Bunnings Warehouse, a national hardware retail chain, has been one of the nation's great success stories over the past decade. In a period of remarkable growth between 1993 and 2019 they came from virtually nowhere to become one of Australia's most valuable brands and one of its most profitable businesses.

They established a reputation for investing in their people and especially for developing breakthrough leaders at all levels in the business. They are clear that the seeds to their success lie in empowerment at the frontline as well as their ability to build a team-based culture in every store. They not only refer to each of their employees as team members, but their vision expresses that it is "our teams that make it happen".

Peter Davis formerly Managing Director, believed in keeping it simple and investing in people. He believes:

"Retail is a very hands-on business and you can't do that by building bureaucracies with a lot of control mechanisms. To have affinity with your team and to understand the demands of the shop floor are certainly the key to success for a leader."

Willem Pruys, their first National Human Resources Manager, believes it was the significant investment in the self-esteem of their workforce that has paid considerable dividends and has given them a distinctive edge in productivity and performance. He believed that this investment in self-esteem delivered a distinctive style of leadership. It is a style that is performance oriented, yet personal, and it uses both empowerment and transformation to bring out the best in their people. Bunnings developed leaders who are skilled in breakthrough leadership or high involvement leadership as it is termed there.

Martin Duffy who was responsible for organisational and capability development saw his role as building systems and processes that develop the capability that is inherent within each team member. He believed that recruiting good people is just the start and that it is really how their leaders bring out their potential that turns them into proven performers. Duffy believed that his challenge was to create an environment in which the leaders and their teams took personal responsibility for their own learning and development. Developing broad leadership capability is a key strategic imperative for Bunnings and is regarded as a distinctive capability which has driven their remarkable success.

Bunnings has a leadership model which is built around personal leadership behaviours and is aimed at developing the potential of people. They have identified five key capabilities that high involvement leaders use in developing their people. Those capabilities are building trust, inspiring action, developing potential, driving performance and bringing the vision to life.

Bunnings Leadership Model

For the leaders to bring out the best in their people, they must first build trust and inspire action. On this foundation they can then develop people and drive their performance. Leaders at all levels are taken through workshops where through debate and challenge they reach shared agreement on the personal behaviours associated with these capabilities. Once this is done, they can then be peer coached to develop action plans which will enable them to consistently display them.

For example, the behaviours associated with building trust might be leading by example and acting with integrity. Inspiring action might involve speaking with conviction and passion and strategically setting goals. Developing people might include creating a caring and enjoyable environment and empowering team members to take ownership. Driving performance might come from defining challenging yet achievable goals and monitoring and communicating progress. Once these behaviours are identified personally then the expectation is on the leader to put them into action.

Bunnings Leadership Behaviours

This company's success is built around the belief that it is what a person actually does that makes the difference and that it is what their leaders do with them that determines how much of their potential is realised. Developing people, building culture and providing an exceptional experience for customers and being able to do this consistently across stores and locations, especially during a period of rapid growth, has been a remarkable achievement for this company.

If the hidden value in companies is the undeveloped potential of employees, then it is companies like Bunnings which are going to benefit in this new world. Companies with old mindsets who treat their people as commodities, as simply employees, cannot compete with those companies who regard their people as assets and the development of their potential as their true source of sustainable competitive advantage.

Building strong teams, bringing out the best in people and then developing them effectively, are leadership skills of the new era. Many companies aspire to it, more have the right intent, but few actually have the insight and the discipline to bring it to life in their culture.

Inspiration and Engagement

Breakthrough leadership takes inspiration, and translates it into the simple behaviours that leaders exhibit in all of their daily interactions with their people. It challenges mindsets and tackles the psychological impediments to change.

It is quite similar to the behaviors that Gallup discovered managers need to exhibit to produce greater levels of engagement in their teams. Gallup's research has shown that the root of employee disengagement is poor management. Their research reveals that managers can raise employee engagement by doing four basic things:

1. Clearly communicate expectations
2. Put people in roles where they can use their strengths
3. Provide feedback
4. Give people the sense that they are cared for

Marcus Buckingham an international expert in employee engagement and management development, has identified the four things that great managers do as:

1. Select good people
2. Define clear expectations
3. Give praise and recognition
4. Show they care for people

He points out that "to manage effectively you must genuinely care about the well being and success of each of your people". He also cautions that "fake care is worse than not caring at all". This is a reinforcement of the critical importance of showing a genuine interest in the development of people and once more highlights that this attribute is at the foundation of the breakthrough experience.

Marcus Buckingham and his associate Ashley Goodall in their book, "Nine Lies About work: a free thinking leader's guide to the real world" write that there is a paradox at work and that is that many of the ideas and practices that are held as settled truths are unhelpful for the people they are intended to serve and are not reflective about what we know about human performance, nor produce the results we are after.

"Each human's nature is unique and managers too often generalize human behavior and our individuality is lost. Our uniqueness is not a flaw, it is the raw material for all healthy, ethical, thriving organisations. Everyone has their own story and unique potential and finding the humanity in the person is the beginning of guiding and appreciating their talent."

They conclude that we have processes and programs for uniformity and conformity, but these rob us of what we really want, which is igniting the human spirit and nurturing the sparks of human distinctiveness.

The Gallup Research has shown over time that the level of employee engagement is strongly related to organisational success. This is the dividend for companies in a competitive sense when they invest in their leadership bench-strength. Developing better leaders makes sound commercial sense. Better leaders build better cultures and build stronger relationships with their people. This directly leads to higher levels of engagement and it is this more intense engagement which enables breakthrough leaders to inspire people to go beyond what they might think is possible and thus make a greater contribution through their work.

The sad truth is that for many workers, and it may be the majority in many workplaces, find in their daily reality that they are led by managers who are at best mediocre and at worse are destructive. These managers, far from motivating them, are more likely to de-motivate, and far from inspiring, are more likely to suck the life from people. This is unfortunately still the sad reality for too many and the truth is that it is not so hard for managers to fix.

If a person accepts a leadership role then it is fair to expect that he or she will lead. It becomes part of a professional obligation. Given the impact that leaders have for good or for bad, it is too important to be neglected or to be left to the personal inclination of each manager. The minimum expectation should be at least that they do no harm. Managers can do so much more to develop their people when they put their mind to it, and when they have their heart in it and when they possess some basic leadership skills.

In general people join a company, but leave their boss. It is common practice that the best people are attracted by an organisation's reputation or the brand, but often leave disappointed by the treatment they receive. Poor managers at best force people out quickly. This at least enables them to look for a place to work where their talents will be appreciated and developed. Unfortunately, however, many people stay working for poor managers and in the process become dispirited and disengaged. They close down their feelings and they learn not to expect too much. In this way they protect themselves against the psychological anxiety and pain that occurs when there is a dissonance between their beliefs and the reality of their situation.

It is a form of psychological abuse when managers ignore their people and systematically undermine their confidence and self-belief. Many managers would do this by neglect, some because of incompetence, others because they are concentrating on satisfying their own ego needs. True leadership is not self-serving; it has to be directed towards the service of others. The best managers express their commitment to leadership when they inspire their followers and work to development their potential.

Clearly inspiration can be stimulated by the power of the vision, the significance of a person's work in contributing towards that vision, and the nature of the relationship they have with their manager. Breaking through old ways of thinking and behaving can have a direct and immediate impact on a person's motivation and development. This is sustained by the nature of the relationship with the leader over time, but this process is reinforced by a deeper satisfaction of some basic inner needs that exist within all of us. It is the satisfaction of these basic human needs or drives that builds the resilience required to deal with adversity, and to persist with change over the long haul. These needs are tapped into by leaders who are able to understand at a deeper level that what drives each individual is a longing for significance and a yearning for success. The sad reality is that for many people, they may have experienced years of indifferent management which has dampened their belief and their hope. Basic needs when they are met, leave a person feeling satisfied and motivated and needs when they are not met leave a person frustrated and dissatisfied.

Inspiration and Need Satisfaction

Much of what a breakthrough leader does through the interaction with followers is intended to change thinking, but it also has the consequence of satisfying needs. In this way it contributes to the on-going motivation of each person. How the leader treats the follower, and the work experience that is provided, have a significant impact on the satisfaction of some fundamental human needs. Breakthrough leaders through their respect for people, and their belief in their potential, create an environment which is conducive to the satisfaction of some basic human needs. When these needs are satisfied people feel more satisfied and are more motivated to perform.

The need for service is best met when people feel that they make a difference to the lives of others and contribute to something that has a deeper purpose. Their motivational driver is toward serving others and to making the world a better place. When they can see that what they do makes a contribution to the wider community in which they live, they then feel a great sense of satisfaction in their work. Many people work for charities or not-for-profits because they are motivated by this need. Some dedicate their lives to the service of others, independent of any financial rewards that they might, or more typically might not, receive. The need to contribute finds its greatest satisfaction when there is a close alignment between a person's vision and values and the vision and values of the organisation.

For many this passion is expressed through service to customers and the opportunity to make a difference to them and their lives. These people derive great satisfaction by solving problems for customers and other stakeholders. This need finds its greatest satisfaction when the products and services provided for the customer deliver real and tangible benefits. Whilst this is closely related to the need to contribute, the sense of contribution tends to be more of a "big picture" issue whereas service is more immediate and more about a direct personal impact.

Many people are passionate about their teams and colleagues and their work brings them friendship and belonging. This sense of belonging is one of the most basic of all human needs and is a reflection that humans are essentially social creatures and so for many people work is more than a job it is also an important set of personal relationships. Friendship is often a major reason why people stay in their job and choose not to leave when offered greater opportunities elsewhere. This need finds its greatest expression in teamwork and in highly collaborative cultures.

Many people have a passion for autonomy and work best when they have high levels of freedom and independence and when they can take ownership and use their initiative. This is most pronounced in the professional services and in knowledge work, where there is substantial resistance to micro-management. Technical specialists and workers with significant expertise tend to value high levels of autonomy and often have to be persuaded to trade off some independence for the sake of the team.

Some people have a strong achievement drive and they are most satisfied in work that brings mastery and success and delivers associated rewards. This basic human need is seen in human development through competitiveness and the drive to win. These are people, attracted by recognition and rewards and who measure their progress by some external measure such as the position they hold and the benefits that they receive. They are often most attracted by strong leadership and find their greatest satisfaction when working in cultures that are meritocracies.

Another need is for personal development and these people are attracted by work which provides challenge, learning and career development. These people believe that their career success will be built upon their own increased capabilities. If they are not learning they feel that they are being left behind. Breakthrough leaders constantly look for opportunities which might challenge these workers and seek to provide experiences which provide the stretch that they seek.

The need for security might be expressed through a desire for predictability, consistency and safety. This in many ways is possibly the most basic of all human needs and it is the one that the high structure, command and control organisations most effectively harnessed. In today's world increasing numbers of workers appreciate that this need will be best satisfied through making themselves more employable and as a consequence they will feel more satisfied when working with a leader who provides not only support but also skill development.

The need for recognition is best satisfied by leaders who provide feedback and appreciation. Breakthrough leaders use the power of recognition to build self-esteem and provide consistent constructive feedback to build capability. Putting the spotlight on the follower's achievements and building his or her professional reputation is a significant motivational factor for people who have a need for recognition. This has the opposite effect to the criticism which is still so widely used by poor managers in the misguided belief that it is an effective motivational tool, but which in reality undermines confidence, builds resentment and reduces self-esteem.

Those who seek pride through their work might look for a job with prestige and a chance to be respected. This need is tapped into by the military with their regard for uniform and their respect for tradition. Most people at some level want to work for an organisation that is respected within the community and the pride that they experience is a major source of motivation for them. Thus, the brand and reputation within the industry, or within the community, becomes an important factor in recruitment

There are people also who need power and seek roles where can make decisions and exercise control. Breakthrough leaders help them to appreciate what they can and can't control and how to use influence to balance a strong power drive. They also can challenge them to understand that for leaders who are change agents, the best way to satisfy a need for power comes from working through people, not working over people. A drive for power can be a strong force for change but is most effective when directed as part of a team in today's more collaborative workplaces.

Understanding human psychology and what motivates and drives, as well as inhibits and blocks, the people who are led, is the hallmark of a true breakthrough leader. They understand that the breakthrough process is always personal and requires a deep understanding of what each person is looking for from their work. It is through satisfying these needs that enthusiasm is sustained in the long run and a leader can never do this if he or she does not, as a starting point, show a genuine interest in the development of each person in the team.

Satisfying these needs is a personal drive for the follower, and a professional requirement for the skilled leader. Intrinsic motivation which is derived from internal need satisfaction becomes a self-generating energising force. The astute leader understands that when this is applied in combination with breakthrough leadership, then people are more likely to make breakthroughs in their development.

There is little doubt that how you treat people has an effect on their mood and motivation, and then ultimately on their aspiration and achievement. When people are filled with doubt and lack confidence, they look for daily attention and reassurance. When they are self-motivated, they require less support. The foundation for a strong relationship between leaders and followers is trust and trust is built upon the perceived integrity of the leader. Without integrity and trust the leader cannot make the emotional connection required to build deeper relationship with others.

When leaders are seen to have integrity in what they say and do, they build the trust necessary to create genuine understanding. It is this genuine understanding that enables leaders to find the spark that will ignite inspiration for each member of the team. It is trust and satisfaction of needs which makes the relationship endure.

Chapter 10

Redefining Success

How the success factors have shifted

The factors that once led to organisational success are no longer those that produce success today. Our definitions of what it means to be successful have shifted. Whereas it was once acceptable to define success in terms of size, that is no longer true today. Growth for the sake of growth can be a liability. Today business is looking for profitable growth as the only long-term sustainable solution. Offering people jobs for life is no longer realistic. Now it is about providing challenge and learning and opportunities for development. Nor would customers be satisfied, as they once were, with just receiving a product or service. Today customers are demanding an experience, a relationship, even a partnership and they certainly want satisfaction to be defined on their terms. Investors too want more. Marginal returns on investments are no longer sufficient to attract global capital, and even individual investors are more careful to assess their total shareholder return.

In the quest for growth and value, companies are continually looking to external factors (especially mergers and acquisitions) and internal factors (organic growth and innovation) to meet the demand. Driving organisational strategy has been a distinctive shift in the factors that underpin success.

Shifting Organisational Success Factors

In the past, the drivers of success were likely to be:-

Control – top down direction with command and control management.

Dependence – workers dependent on their bosses for information, instructions and approval.

Hierarchy – many levels of decision-making and formal power and authority.

Standardised – reduce variation to drive consistency in process.

Predictable – a "no surprises" culture.

Management – focus more on the task, less on the people.

These factors were created in a climate of business as usual and brought success when all strategies were basically "more of the same". The traditional industrial organisation was designed to get required effort which meant people doing their job, as they were told, when they were told. Many in the workforce adapted quite well to this environment where there was little demand to think for oneself and to use initiative. The focus was the job and all too often it simply meant keeping the boss happy. This corresponded to the development of a silo culture with a "not my job", "not my problem" mentality. People were paid for attendance rather than performance. They were paid for the hours put in, not the outcomes personally achieved. It was not effort that was rewarded, but attendance.

In this environment, management rather than leadership was called for. Management with a focus on supervision, (of others' work), on the task (the work to be done), and on problem solving (quickly rectifying mistakes made). Promotion was based on seniority rather than merit. Reliability and adherence to rules and procedures was the key performance indicator. New recruits understood that the first priority was to learn how to fit in and then to do what was expected. These were cultures with rules driven values, the opposite of the values driven rules that are desired today.

These were administrative cultures which got consistency and predictability but which were also remarkably underperforming by today's standards. They created cultures with little pressure to excel and low demands to achieve. Conformity was valued over performance and predictability over initiative. They had little interest in unlocking human potential, and had no regard for energising and motivating what in most cases was a largely disengaged workforce. The job of the manager was to direct the workforce, not to engage people. It was primarily to control behaviour, not to build trust.

With the growth of a more globalized market and a highly competitive landscape however, being good enough was no longer sufficient and the era of the performance culture arrived. What it required was a complete rethinking of the human factor in organisational success. What it led to was a fundamental re-assessment of the critical factors that drive success.

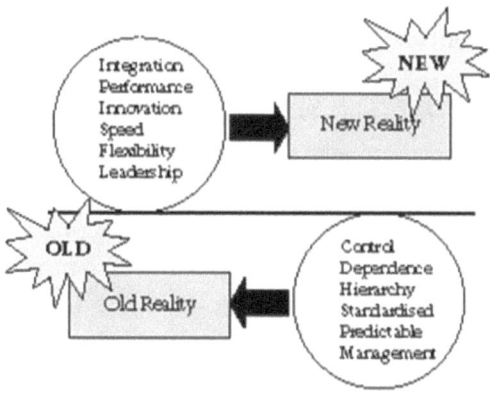

Changing Success Factors

The New Success Factors

The new characteristics that were seen to drive success were more likely to be:

> *Integration* – breaking down silos and building processes for collaboration.

> *Performance* – creating a culture with clear focus on results with targets and measures for achievement.

> *Innovation* – constantly challenging the status quo and looking for a better way

> *Speed* – fast decision-making and a reduction in bureaucracy

> *Flexibility* – the ability to be highly adaptable according to customer need or strategic requirement

> *Leadership* – using shared vision and shared values to drive alignment, focus and engagement

The goal is to build an organisation which maximises these key success factors. The key is to find those who can add most value and enable them to collaborate to achieve superior performance. The old success factors become a liability when the game rapidly changes and the way we measure success and failure shifts. In the boundaryless organisation, which was the conceptual framework applied in General Electric under Jack Welch, "the old success factors needed to be combined with a new and sometimes paradoxical set of factors that look very different from the old".

When these success factors rapidly shift, the organisational response has to be likewise swift. The old success factors were driven by an entrenched managerial mindset and were nurtured by what in today's thinking is an antiquated view of human performance. Their intent was to minimise the impact of the human variable and to reduce the influence of the individual in particular.

New Workplaces and New Cultures

The new success factors require a new type of employee; someone who is confident, capable, courageous and guided by conviction. Whilst the old factors relied on structure, the new factors rely upon culture.

Integration is embedded when there is a focus on co-ordination and cross functional processes and systems. This requires cultures that value collaboration and leaders who are collegial and individuals who are confident to give their opinion and to share their knowledge. These individuals are sensitive to the significance of what they do for others and understand how they contribute to strategic success of the company. They have strong collaborative skills and work with a high degree of interdependence.

Performance is nurtured in cultures that value achievement and have comprehensive processes that build new capability in individuals who are committed to life-long learning and the development of potential. The best performing teams have moved beyond simple participation as the goal to contribution which recognises that the most effective team members are those who make the greatest contribution to the team result. This requires individuals who are not only capable, but are also confident of the contribution they make.

Innovation thrives in cultures that value learning and initiative and where there is a climate which encourages people to have their say and to constantly strive to find better ways to do things. These are cultures which reduce the risk involved in making a mistake and replace blame with learning as the response to failure. This requires individuals with the courage to take a stand and speak up, and who have the confidence to challenge the status quo.

Speed is fostered in cultures which drive out bureaucracy and which simplify decision making. The nimbleness of the small entrepreneurial firm is eagerly sought by big corporations and this requires individuals who seek empowerment, ownership and accountability. This works best with individuals who work with a deep sense of purpose and who put group interest ahead of self-interest.

Flexibility flows from cultures that are adaptable and which value variation in processes and procedures as a strategic capability. These are cultures which start from the customer's perspective and which encourage employees to develop deep customer mindsets. This suits workers who prefer to be guided by principles rather than fixed procedures, and who can learn quickly and act promptly to meet customer needs. This requires individuals who will take ownership and it is this ownership that gives them the courage to take a stand and to be strong customer advocates. It works best with individuals who have the confidence to cope with ambiguity and to take responsibility and to make decisions even when faced with uncertainty.

Leadership is best developed in cultures where leaders are supported and where leadership is regarded as a distinctive competitive advantage. It is an attribute of the organisation, not just the individual and this capability is best established with an inclusive and democratic approach to leadership development. In these organisations leadership is seen not as a position but as a core human capability which sees leadership as anything that anyone does that helps the team or the company to succeed. It requires individuals who see themselves as both followers, and leaders when it is their moment to step into the game. In this sense all members of the company are at times followers and at times leaders. This works best with individuals who have the confidence, capability and courage to contribute and the strong commitment to team success.

In any organisation strategy is built upon capability which in turn rests upon the collective ability of the people concerned. Any one can change strategy as an intellectual exercise, but its realisation is totally dependent upon capability or the rapid development of required capability. Irrespective of how an organisation promotes itself, or markets itself it is not the words but the customer's actual experience which determines strategic effectiveness.

A business might promote a shift to customer service as its prime strategy but this would be meaningless without the ability to recruit the right people and then deploy them effectively. It also depends on the ability to provide a consistent level of service and the willingness to monitor the customer experience closely.

A major part of competitive advantage today is accelerating capability development. As John Hagel and John Seely Brown write:

> "traditional strategies today are less effective.... developing talent is where the value will come from.... the competitive edge ultimately depends on the firms institutional capacity to accelerate learning across enterprise boundaries, rather than simply mobilising static resources".

This is a very dynamic view of strategic advantage and it places a considerable onus on the ability of leaders at all levels to nurture the development of talent and to bring out the potential of the workforce. This is really the role of transformational leaders and especially of breakthrough leaders. This will require leaders who are skilled in working with both human ability and human attitude and who can maximise both to deliver agility as well as performance.

Ability rests upon the application of talent, whereas attitude rests upon the application of commitment. A key indicator of commitment is the amount of discretionary effort displayed by the workforce at all levels. Discretionary effort thrives in a culture where people are prepared to do more than they are required to do, or even more than they are paid to do and in a culture with strong engagement.

Discretionary effort rests upon the nature of the psychological contract between employee and employer. In this contract there is an understanding that employees have the freedom and autonomy to do their work in their own way and the employer in return is given their contribution and effort. It is where employees are valued and given recognition and the employer in return receives increased effort and commitment. This is the pathway to superior performance and it is a pathway that the world's best organisations take on their journey to excellence. The best in the world build cultures with high levels of commitment and engagement, and their people continually deliver above expectations.

The Challenge of Discretionary Effort

John Purcell and a team from the University of Bath in the United Kingdom, over a long period studied discretionary effort and the impact of management on team performance. His particular focus was to understand the extra effort that some workers put in to lift performance and to understand why some companies were good at getting people to go the extra mile.

Purcell identified eleven key policy areas that drive discretionary effort:

1. Teamwork
2. Career development
3. Job challenge
4. Job security
5. Involvement
6. Communication
7. Job autonomy
8. Work/life balance
9. Pay satisfaction
10. Training and development
11. Performance appraisal

His work revealed that all of these factors influence a worker's ability and motivation to participate. He reported that in the end, the more workers feel a part of the company, the better is their performance. The policy areas identified are those that directly impact upon an employee's sense of involvement and feeling of importance.

The critical ingredient in this mix however is the ability of managers, supervisors and team leaders to bring these policies to life. It is not the policies themselves, but the way that they are implemented that is the key. Variation in performance occurs when there is variation in manager application.

Purcell's summary was that:

> "In the end the more workers feel part of the company, the better is their performance. Yet there is often great variation in performance across the same company. The difference is often in the ability of line managers to learn how to apply policy to motivate staff and give them a real opportunity. The role of the line manager or team leader is to enhance workers' commitment and job satisfaction. However, some managers can't always be relied upon to properly engage policy or to play by the rules, and so performance outcomes vary."

What Purcell described is the essence of breakthrough leadership. Leaders who bring policies to life, build involvement and display a personal interest in their people and their development. In areas of an organisation where cynicism is endemic and disappointment is more entrenched, it is only through leaders who display breakthrough behaviours that these mindsets can be changed.

The challenge is to change mindsets at all levels and to create the conditions whereby individuals can grow and develop, confront their own uncertainties and fears and take the path towards realising their own potential. This is the ultimate in discretionary effort. It is the step beyond simply having a positive attitude towards work, to the step where people discover the motivation and meaning which produces real fulfilment through work. It is the task of leaders today to create workplaces which deliver on human potential.

Organisations can no longer compete effectively on the basis of required effort. People doing only that which they are required to do can never win against teams of people, who are passionate about performance and success. That is certainly a competitive edge for today and so the best organisations globally are investing time and energy in building cultures which increase the engagement of the total workforce. The long-term sustainable advantage is best delivered through the on-going development and engagement of the people.

Moving From Performance to Potential

Moving people from simply doing what is required to delivering beyond the basics is certainly a significant leadership achievement. Greater still is the achievement of leaders who shift people beyond attitude to self-belief and the continued development of their potential. This is the real hidden value in organisations that was described by Charles O'Reilly and Jeffrey Pfeiffer from Stanford University. Their research looked at how great companies are able to achieve extraordinary results with ordinary people. They studied two questions:

1.   Why are some companies able to sustain long term success?
2.   Why don't their competitors copy them?

In their book, "Hidden Value: how great companies achieve extraordinary results with ordinary people", O'Reilly and Pfeffer looked at a number of long term successful global companies to understand what drives their success and to understand why their competitors don't simply copy them. The message from the hidden value research is that the best don't succeed simply because they get the best people, rather it's because they get the best out of the people they get. As O'Reilly and Pfeffer report: "there is a real, sustainable competitive advantage to be had in unleashing the potential in a company's workforce – an advantage that competitors cannot easily imitate even when they understand exactly what you are doing."

In looking at globally successful companies they found that the secret of their success was that they had been able to build companies which enabled "ordinary people to behave like stars". They were able to achieve sustained success because they then had embedded the success factors into their systems and processes. In other words, they built corporate cultures which supported long term success.

In this way they suggested that the source of sustainable competitive advantage exists within every company. It is about creating an environment where people can thrive and then sending a clear message through the values, strategy and vision that people and their development is their real source of that advantage. It is up to the leaders at all levels to bring this hidden value within people out. These are companies with a tremendous capacity to harvest discretionary effort.

The breakthrough component here is often the interface between discretionary effort and conviction. Helping people to find the work they really enjoy, to find their real passion and to find the cause they truly want to pursue is a real service that leaders provide to their followers.

No longer is it just a job. The opportunity exists today as never before for people to find fulfilment through their work. It is for leaders to show them the significance in what they do and to remove the impediments to their development. Working in a job you truly enjoy and where you are treated with respect, can produce a good attitude. Finding a purpose that inspires your work is to find the source of deep conviction. This is a step beyond discretionary effort, to a deep commitment to making a difference through work. Making a difference to our teams, our communities and the people we serve. This is the real leadership gift.

Good management practices can get required effort from people. This is the effort people need to put into their jobs in order to do their jobs and keep their jobs. Command and control managers who focus on simple compliance, invariably get little more than required effort. They tend to act as if they believe that what you think, how you feel, and what you might be capable of, has less relevance than what you do.

This was the environment that pertained prior to the "knowledge revolution" where manual labour was the commodity in demand. Good organisations operating in this mode were able to get satisfactory performance outcomes through the application of highly structured performance management systems. These systems were designed to focus human activity and to tie human behaviour closely to a consequence.

These techniques, whilst effective in their time, do not produce significant psychological engagement or discretionary effort. Discretionary effort is a personal choice. It is what an individual chooses to bring to work. It cannot be demanded or commanded because it is dependent upon what each person thinks and feels and no one other than the person concerned can know that. It is essentially the act of a volunteer.

Discretionary effort is an attitude based on two fundamentals:

Feeling – that I enjoy what I do and it makes a difference to the result.

Thinking – that what we do is worth doing and contributes to a greater good.

Whilst obtaining required effort can be achieved through management, achieving discretionary effort is derived through leadership. It is leadership which unlocks human potential and creates the environment where people feel motivated and inspired. It is the breakthrough experience which creates the conditions where people challenge themselves and grow in confidence.

The organisations that excel are those that receive the greatest amount of discretionary effort by the greatest number of people, for the longest period of time. These are organisations which create cultures of engagement whereby people bring their passion, their energy and their commitment to work on a daily basis. The best value this capability and treat it as an essential part of their identity.

The new frontier for these companies is going beyond discretionary effort to tap into the conviction of their people. This takes them beyond energy and passion and beyond attitude into the field of purpose and belief.

Peter Senge, author of the classic management book, "The Fifth Discipline", promotes learning and purpose as key drivers of business success. He writes that "the success of an enterprise depends on the spirit and intelligence of people, and you can't tap that if you pretend that the purpose is making money, because not that many people care. They care a little, but not a lot. And if the organisation doesn't stand for something that means something, you don't get their inventiveness, their patience, their perseverance, their commitment."

Conviction is tapped when an organisation is able to inspire people through the power of purpose and this happens when it is able to show people how through their work, they can make a difference to their colleagues, their customers, and the communities in which they live.

The Roots of Competitive Advantage

Competitive advantage is created by building distinctive capability and then aligning personal vision and values and an organisation's vision and values. Breakthrough leaders, because of their insight into how their people think, are in a better position to be able to do this effectively and sensitively. Most people want to make a difference, to have an impact or to leave their mark. The best organisations are able to uncover what it is that will bring significance to each person's work and to better understand what it is that each individual truly wants to achieve.

A company driven by purpose and built upon the contribution of individuals strongly committed to that purpose is a powerful force. The successful companies in future will be those which can move beyond discretionary effort to unlock the full potential of their people.

That is why leadership skills which remove the impediments to individual development will be sought after and leaders who can apply these skills at a personal level to the development of their people will be in demand. The "hidden value" in organisations is in attracting good people and making them even better.

The leadership challenge will not be about mobilising more people, but rather getting more from the people that are mobilised. In an era of resource constraints and productivity hurdles, it will be the ability of organisations and leaders to unlock human potential which will be the key. The real test of leadership will be measured by the impact on people. The question that every leader should ask is this: are your people better off for being led by you?

This will require leaders who can build shared vision as a major tool of inspiration. They will need a clearly defined strategy which team members can translate into their own personal priorities and a strong performance culture which supports the development of each team member. Ultimately it requires organisations to have leaders at all levels who are breakthrough leaders, who are skilled in mindset change. These will be leaders who can bring psychology to performance to remove the impediments both personal and institutional to the development of human potential.

The new success factors in competitive strategy demand a rethink of competitive advantage. It opens the doors for leaders with a more sophisticated understanding of human psychology than that displayed by leaders in the past. They will be challenged to build cultures which nurture talent and unfold potential.

No longer can we have structures which undermine human achievement and procedures which destroy motivation. This is a world beyond the quest for knowledge alone, to one where knowledge and imagination are both in demand. That we can manage behaviour will be a given; the leadership edge will now be in developing potential.

Children as they grow have no choice but to learn. We have to find ways to continue this process into our world of work. Understanding what stops human development will be a significant advance. Removing the impediments will be a significant achievement.

Breakthrough leaders will facilitate this process, and in so doing, will help each employee to develop to his or her personal best. By doing this, these leaders will make their greatest contribution to the ultimate, long term, sustainable success of the organisations and customers they serve.

Chapter 11

Developing Breakthrough Leaders

A new approach to developing leaders

The skills of breakthrough leadership are not the skills required by the few. It is not simply for the executive ranks, nor is it for exclusive programs designed for high potential leaders. These skills are too important to be exclusive. They are the attributes that leaders at all levels, in all situations need to possess. The behaviours described that drive the breakthrough process, need to be developed in all leaders. If not already, they will soon become a pre-requisite for effective leadership.

Leaders have a great opportunity and a profound responsibility. They can lead their followers into the future, developing them in the process or they can leave them as they found them. In practical terms the major thing standing between the people and their future is their leader. Some leaders put in the time to bring out the best in all of the people that they lead. Other leaders neglect this responsibility and so restrict the future opportunities available to their people. They don't put in the time to truly understand each person and so never build the trust and the shared vision so crucial to the development process.

All leaders have a responsibility to develop their people. Along with building performance and creating shared vision, developing people is a fundamental of leadership. It is also a fundamental that is too important to be left to chance. All leaders need to be given the skills required to breakthrough barriers to development.

The New Leadership Challenge

To be at their best people need to be confident and capable, have the courage to challenge and be driven by a deep sense of personal conviction. To be truly effective the leaders need to appreciate the role they play in developing these characteristics in people and incorporate the breakthrough capabilities into their leadership repertoire.

A good starting point for leaders would be to understand what it means to show a genuine interest in the development of each person they lead. How this priority is established and how the time discipline is built into their daily practice is a key consideration. They need to be skilled in listening and asking the other person for input. They need to understand the difference between delegation and empowerment and how to create the framework whereby they can have control without being controlling. They need to know how to set an appropriate challenge and build the confidence in the individual that the challenge is achievable. They need to be skilled in the basics of coaching and support. Finally, they need to appreciate the importance of feedback and recognition and be able to do both especially during times of adversity.

In addition to these behaviours they also need to create the focus and alignment necessary for strategic success. There are specific capabilities relevant to each industry and to each market environment which are necessary for competitive success. But at the heart of these specialised skills and strategies are the personal attributes that enable each person to overcome the self-limiting thinking that so often restricts development.

Some people fail to achieve their potential because they are not suited to a particular job, or because of a personality clash with a boss, or because of relationship issues with colleagues. These are specific situations which require specific action to resolve the problem. The majority of people, however, under-perform for four main reasons:-

1. Attitude problems which can have a *thinking* and/or a *feeling* component.
2. Ability problems related to talent or aptitude
3. Sustainability problems resulting from low resilience or lack of support.
4. Context factors stemming from workplace relationships or the nature of the workplace itself.

In each of these cases breakthrough leaders have a role to play. Working on mindset, or self-belief, will be the best way to deal with impediments that are of a cognitive or thinking nature. Working on motivation or uncovering needs will be the best way to deal with impediments that are in the affective or feeling domain.

Breakthrough leaders may also work on competence or knowledge if the impediment is one of talent, or provide support for learning and access to development if the impediment is related to aptitude. Building resilience involves managing stress and developing learned optimism. Imagination needs to flourish through the stimulation of ideas and dreams.

If the impediments are related to the context within which work takes place, then building trusted relationships or increasing networks may be the best intervention. Leaders have the ability to identify or create career opportunities and to balance these with the life stage needs of their followers. In this way they can ensure that the workplace is as conducive as possible to their continued growth and development of each person.

Breakthrough leadership is a significant investment in the self-esteem of others. It is about satisfying their needs to be valued and to be appreciated. It is about giving them the confidence to seek opportunities and the courage to speak up and challenge themselves. With their self-esteem enhanced, they can then put energy into building the capabilities necessary for success in their professional lives. Their belief in the worth of what they do then brings a sense of purpose which drives and sustains their commitment.

All leaders need the breakthrough skills which are personal and interpersonal and the strategic skills which are professional. It is too important to be left to chance. All of this needs a concerted approach to developing leadership and to equipping leaders with skills necessary for success.

There are seven core techniques which can form the basis of a comprehensive leadership development process:-

1. Modelling
2. Life experience
3. Development
4. Self-awareness
5. Self-management
6. Context
7. Support

Modelling

By far and away the most effective method of developing leaders is through the impact of excellent role models. When budding leaders are surrounded by excellent leaders, some of their influence rubs off through the process of identification. It is well established in developmental psychology that much of what a child learns comes not from direct instruction, but from watching and copying the behaviour of significant adults in their environment.

Young leaders are similarly greatly influenced by the leadership models that they are exposed to throughout their career. Participants in the research outlined in this book spoke of leaders who had inspired them at all stages in their career, but often the ones who had the greatest impact were the role models early in a career.

Unfortunately, a number of participants could only report negative role models and suggested that it was this experience that had inspired them to be different. The problem with a negative experience is that it shows you what you do not want, but it gives few clues as to what would be a positive alternative. A deeper problem however, is that a poor manager early in a career can create cynicism which can have long term self-limiting consequences, especially if the cynicism becomes deeply entrenched by exposure to a culture where cynicism is deeply embedded.

All organisations need to ensure that the managers, supervisors and team leaders, who are leading new recruits, are exemplary role models themselves. If they are not their impact can be long lasting and lock in low personal expectations and self-limiting thinking which can lead to long term under performance. Ensuring that leaders are astute and understand the impact that they have on cultures, teams and individuals, and ensuring that they are committed to building the next generation of leaders is the best direct investment an organisation can make in building leadership capability.

Life Experience

Life experience can also have a huge impact on leadership development. Martin Seligman believes that whether one develops an optimistic or pessimistic explanatory style occurs early in life. Whilst the workplace can do little to change life history, it can do a lot to change the course of life in the future. An understanding of explanatory style (ie. how a person makes sense of and interprets what happens to them) can give people the thinking skills to deal with the self-defeating impact of negative thinking. It can also give them the support required to be able to keep things in perspective and find the positive aspects of a difficult situation. Caring leaders can help to prevent a person's career from becoming a negative self-fulfilling prophesy and instead change the course to a more positive, constructive one. They can help their followers to undertake a more comprehensive analysis of any situation, which includes an assessment of both negative and positive implications.

Leaders can also arrange challenging assignments or projects which provide stretch with support, and provide empowerment balanced by clear accountabilities. Many of the participants in this research had leaders who provided them with experiences which took them out of their comfort zones and helped them to confront self-defeating thinking.

Experiences can also be provided in the broader community as a way of developing leadership potential. An increasing number of organisations encourage their people to undertake some volunteer work during their working hours as a way of exposing them to aspects of life that they would not otherwise encounter. They believe that these life experiences have a broadening impact and help their leaders to develop greater self-awareness of their own personal values and a greater appreciation of the diversity of life experiences in the community.

Development

Whilst it is acknowledged that the most effective leadership development takes place on the job, it is also acknowledged that there is also a role for formal development programs. Executive education is a large part of the offering for international business schools and M.B.A. programs, and executive M.B.A. programs, are still in high demand.

All large global organisations, as well as most large national organisations, would also have their own in-house leadership development programs. Increasingly, these are led by the business leaders themselves, and often delivered in partnership with an external provider. Many of these programs are also supported by customised 360º leadership feedback instruments and by personalised executive coaching sessions. Most of the participants in this research had been involved in a considerable amount of formal leadership development and many had received extensive leadership feedback.

As issues of succession become critical the identification of leadership talent and then programs to develop that potential are now well established. It is common practice for these programs to be built around personal leadership development plans, which are prepared individually and which identify career objectives, goals for improvement and the degree of support required. The majority of participants in this research reported that they had their own leadership development plans and many commented that these were most effective when their individual expectations and goals were not only supported, but heightened, by inspiring leaders. A common aspect of the support given to them was the encouragement by their leaders to take on leadership challenges and most felt that they did a good job in providing them.

Self-Awareness

It is now considered that the foundation for effective leadership is self-awareness. A leader who is not aware of his or her impact can do little to improve it. It is hard to manage something you are not even aware of. Accurate self-awareness is the starting point for change and this means not only awareness of one's current mindset, but also clarity about personal vision and values that are important. Managers in this research, in the main, reported that the leaders who inspired them were self-aware and clear about their own leadership principles and values. It is probable that it was this self-awareness that gave them enough confidence in their own position to listen, and enough courage to act.

Leadership self-awareness can be enhanced through reflection and feedback. A strong feedback culture generated by formal assessment processes and informal personal communication can be a powerful instrument for building self-awareness. When this is combined with a culture that encourages reflective practice, where leaders build in thinking time as part of their daily discipline, then the mechanisms for self-awareness are strongly embedded.

Self-Management

If self-awareness is the first step, then self- management is the second. Understanding yourself, your drives and your values is important, but more important is what you do. The first step can be little more that wishful thinking, without the discipline to deliver. It is execution which drives performance rather than intent. Effective leaders are those who follow through, do what they say they are going to do and deliver on their promises. In a complex, busy world, managing self can be a real challenge.

Participants in this research spoke of their respect for leaders who helped them to establish priorities for action and who added discipline to their action plans by persistence in following up and by scheduling regular meetings and support sessions.

When leaders at all levels are strong on self-management, then the organisation itself will be strong on strategic execution and performance. This capability is built by having clear accountabilities assigned to leadership tasks and by cascading down a systematic action orientation into business planning. When leaders consistently follow through, it sets in place a strong performance ethic which permeates through all aspects of functioning and powerfully influences the capacity to grow more leaders.

Self-management demands that leaders also have the discipline to exercise self-control. It means that leaders use judgement in how they behave. This means their behaviour is not driven by impulse or by self-indulgence, but rather by the strategic requirements of the situation and the outcome desired. Leaders do not just do what they want to do; they choose their behaviour on the basis of what will be most effective in furthering the strategic agenda and obtaining the desired result. The more self-aware leaders are and the greater their ability to self-manage, the more likely it is that their behaviour will be under their control and most effectively directed.

Participants in this research reported that the leaders who inspired them always seemed to have time for them. Presumably the leaders who inspired were no less busy than the average leader and yet they found the time required to "show a genuine interest". They always gave the impression, at least to their followers, that when they were paying attention, they were not distracted by countless other issues which might have been on their mind.

The discipline of self-management enables leaders to effectively manage their time and to allocate time according to their priorities. Accordingly, these leaders are able to ensure that their leadership style is driven by their own intent, and not by the many competing interests of multiple other stakeholders.

Developing leaders who are able to manage themselves and their priorities is a major strategic imperative. Developing leaders who are able to manage themselves and their emotions is a major cultural imperative. Developing an ethic of accountable self-management is a pre-requisite for execution and performance and this will be central to the delivery of effective change projects.

Context

The context within which leadership development takes place will also have an important bearing upon the quality of leaders produced. Breakthrough leaders are best nurtured in a culture which values learning and where development is embedded into established systems and processes.

The knowledge sharing that comes from collaborative relationships enables all individuals to be involved in the learning process, and imbues in leaders a belief that sharing knowledge rather than hoarding knowledge is beneficial for all. This produces leaders who are more inclined to facilitate the flow of information rather than restrict it.

Participants in this research reported that the leaders who inspired them were open; open with them and open to them. They gave the impression that they were curious and interested and that they valued the thoughts and opinions of their followers. They showed through their words and deeds that they believed their followers had potential to improve and through their sustained interest, they displayed a commitment to their growth and development.

Breakthrough leaders also seek to find, and often create, opportunities for their followers. The context within which a company operates will determine the nature of the opportunities that are possible. A global organisation can create more stretch assignments than a domestic one, and a conglomerate can access more cross industry assignments than a single industry company.

One of the best leadership development assignments is working in a different culture and not only managing apart from one's familiar home context, but also leading a culturally diverse team. Nothing makes a leader dig deeper into personal resources than such a step into the unknown. Leaving a familiar environment where one's track record of success has been established is a daunting experience for any leader, but it is the best one for challenging habitual ways of behaving and for making a leader reflect upon the true basis of their leadership expertise. The wider strategic context, and the internal cultural context are important elements in considering the nature, scope and impact of leadership development provided. Breakthrough leaders aware of situational context make use of it to provide both meaning and opportunities for their followers.

Support

The final element in building strong leadership is the degree of support provided for the process. Certainly, senior leadership support is crucial and senior leaders have an important role to play, not only in endorsing the importance of leadership development, but in being role models for the leadership style promoted.

Senior leaders also have an important role to play as ambassadors for the organisation in the wider community and the image that they project externally has a powerful influence on the integrity of the brand itself. The support that they provide for the development of the individuals in their own senior teams also has a significant impact on the leadership climate more broadly. The expectations placed upon them sends a message about the importance they attach to leadership development and the support they are willing to provide in its development to others.

Participants in this research were unequivocal in talking about the importance of the support provided by their leaders. Inspiring leaders gave them the courage, in many instances, to step out of a comfort zone and put in place a safety net which encouraged them to take risks and to try something new. Support is fundamental to leadership, and followers without the support of their leader are left confused about direction and uncertain about the role that they play. Astute leaders understand the positive and negative aspects of support. Too much can overwhelm and create unhealthy dependency, whereas too little can reduce trust and lead to insecurity.

As a critical foundation for the breakthrough process, leaders need to be able to supply support in the right measure and at the right time. The idea is not to create dependency upon the leader to come up with the answers and to solve problems, but to provide support as insurance against risk and to remove the debilitating threat of blame when mistakes occur. Breakthrough leaders don't cover up mistakes made, but use them as an examples for learning and as a stimulus for personal development.

The Need for Breakthrough Leaders

Developing leaders is a significant challenge for organisations globally and especially for those with substantial growth aspirations. Having enough leaders to lead and manage growth is not a challenge to be underestimated and in a strategic sense the lack of such leaders is the greatest impediment to success. Leadership then is not simply about having more people, but rather getting more from the people. This then calls for a specific type of leadership, not a generic style, but one tailored to the needs of the organization and its social context.

Breakthrough leaders see that core part of their professional responsibility is to develop more leaders. They are driven to help others to grow, learn and develop, and they are skilled at dealing with the self-limiting and self-defeating thinking which is a major impediment to this growth. Building the capability to do this effectively will be a significant competitive advantage. It will be a competitive advantage because not many companies have the discipline to build unique leadership capability, and even fewer have systematic processes to equip their leaders with the skills required.

Most companies are still better at rhetoric than practice, and many are still driven more by politics and the personal agendas of their executives than the vision and strategy espoused by the executive team. This is especially so when executive remuneration is tied to short term business results rather than long term strategic positioning, and it becomes acute when senior leaders are prized more for their own decisiveness and determination rather than for their ability to bring people with them and to advance the team.

Organisations need an accurate assessment of their breakthrough leadership bench strength. Knowing current reality then, and appreciating the gap between that and the vision, gives a good indication of the magnitude of the challenge. A good starting point in the development of breakthrough leadership skills is for leaders at all levels, but especially those in frontline and team leadership roles, to do a comprehensive self-assessment. It is best to start with the leaders closer to the frontline because they have the initial impact on new recruits and because so much of their role should be building teams.

At some stage this has to involve senior leaders as they are the most powerful role models for the broader culture and they are crucial in creating shared vision and strategic alignment with teams across the business. Pushing shared vision down to the front line builds the foundation for a deeper shared purpose to act as a source of inspiration for all. This in turn can provide a powerful connection for bringing significance to the work of individuals at all levels.

Assessing Breakthrough Leadership Capability

Such an assessment can be done by individuals through quiet self-reflection, but it is more effective if carried out through some peer coaching process. Peer coaching involves small groups of leaders coming together for the purpose of individual and collective learning and leadership development. Using a structured tool such as the Breakthrough Leadership Self Assessment Guide can be an effective way for leaders to get useful feedback, mutual support and coaching.

Getting honest, constructive feedback from one's peers requires a high degree of trust and this is most likely to occur when there are no hidden agendas and the common intent is learning and mutual development. A structured peer coaching process can provide the impetus and support necessary for personal change.

Are you a leader who ...	BREAKTHROUGH LEADERSHIP SELF ASSESSMENT	
Takes a genuine interest	1.	Makes regular time to talk with individuals in your team
	2.	Shows real interest in what others are doing
	3.	Displays understanding of the needs of others
Listens and asks for ideas	4.	Asks others about their ideas
	5.	Is an active listener
	6.	Listens patiently to different points of view
Acts on advice	7.	Keeps an open mind and suspends judgment
	8.	Empowers others to do the job
	9.	Encourages others to have their say
Sets a challenge	10.	Seeks challenging assignments and opportunities for others
	11.	Shows confidence in the ability of others to be successful
	12.	Sets stretch goals for others
Provides support and coaching	13.	Builds specific skills and confidence in others
	14.	Follows through on promises
	15.	Provides information and direction others need to do their job
Gives feedback and recognition	16.	Acknowledges efforts and appreciates the achievements of others
	17.	Celebrates success
	18.	Gives personal thanks

Breakthrough Leadership Self Assessment Guide

Step one: begin with an honest self-assessment.

Step two: request feedback from people around you and especially those whose relationship you rely upon to be effective.

Step three: follow up discussions to clarify differences in perception and to solicit suggestions. You don't have to take on board all of the advice you receive, but it is important to show that you are receptive to feedback and open to learning. Remember that stopping doing something may be the best development outcome.

Step four: commit to some change which will improve relationships and make you more effective.

Leaders after they have completed a self-assessment can then review the impact that they are having on followers. If a leader's true effectiveness is to be judged, less by what they do themselves and more by what they cause others to do, then assessing that impact is important. Each follower's development can be reviewed using the Outcomes Self

Assessment as a guide to monitor progress made towards the four key outcomes: confidence, capability, courage and conviction.

The goal is to look for indicators of success in building these four outcomes in individuals and in teams. Key questions could be:-

1. Am I developing the confidence of the people I lead?
2. Am I building the competence of the people I lead?
3. Am I increasing the courage of the people I lead?
4. Am I helping to clarify conviction in the people I lead?

	OUTCOMES SELF ASSESSMENT
Describe yourself	
Confidence	1. Speak up at meetings 2. Look for challenges 3. Have strong self belief 4. Face problems directly / do not avoid responsibility
Capability	5. Are fast learners 6. Keep up to date 7. Are always well prepared 8. Have strong achievement drive
Courage	9. Embrace change 10. Are prepared to challenge what others say 11. Willing to give feedback to others 12. Do the right thing even when it is not popular
Conviction	13. Talk passionately about the job 14. Always have the big picture in mind 15. Have a strong sense of purpose 16. Are proud of what they do

Outcomes Self Assessment

Breakthrough leadership poses a unique leadership challenge, a challenge that requires a new approach to leadership and a new approach to the development of human potential. The organisations that cannot make the shift will struggle to survive. Those that thrive will be those that are not only good for business, but are good for people as well. Exceptional results, and certainly sustainable results, will come through building personal and collective learning capability which is supported by systems and processes for developing people and unlocking hidden value.

Conclusion

Making the Shift to More
Effective Leadership

The times call for a new style of leadership

Leadership does make a difference and it is possible to make the transformation from an organisation which is weak in leadership talent to one where leadership is a competitive and strategic asset. It takes a concentrated effort however, to make this shift in leadership style and capability. You can't become a good leader by accident, it takes significant development and discipline. Some people seem to have naturally some of the attributes of effective leadership. There are those with strong achievement motivation, but with the humility to listen and learn. They may have inherited a head start, but despite any perceived advantage it still needs to be nurtured and brought to fruition by years of disciplined practice. In leadership it is also true as in other areas of life that practice makes perfect.

As organisations gear up to meet the challenges of a highly competitive, rapidly changing world, they will need to face up to four significant shifts in thinking. These are:

1. Given the worldwide talent shortage that is coming, it will not be a matter of getting more people, but of getting more from

the people you have. Many companies squander the talent of the people that they recruit, not knowing how to turn strengths into assets.

2. Since greater discretionary effort, is such a core competitive asset, those firms that can release it will have an edge.

3. Being able to bring a vision to life and shortening the time between idea and implementation are fundamental requirements in the transformational change process and this will depend upon people who are confident, capable and have the courage of their convictions.

4. The best people will be attracted to, and want to stay, in the organisations that are respected in their communities and are driven by a deep sense of purpose and contribution. In the new world of work people are looking not only for the greatest career opportunities, but also the greatest opportunities for personal development.

It is into this people context that the model of breakthrough leadership is best applied. Organisations will not meet these challenges with old ways of thinking and old ways of managing. It is not the management of people, but the development of people, which is the key. In this context, leaders will need to understand psychology and be skilled at helping to remove the impediments that stop people from reaching their potential. Whilst many of these impediments are locked in outmoded systems and processes, many are also locked into the mindsets that we frequently apply when considering life's challenges and opportunities. Breakthrough leadership is not a one step process, it is continual process related to life-long learning where all of us need to break through whatever constraints and impediments are blocking our development. Breakthrough leaders will be change catalysts, providing the inspiration required to breakthrough these layers of resistance.

Finally there are some key points to consider for organisations intent on making the shift to more effective leadership:

1. How people are treated has an effect upon their mood and motivation and ultimately their commitment, contribution and achievement. The performance, including financial performance,

of an organisation will be driven in large measure by the engagement of the broader workforce. Leaders who act with integrity, treat people with respect, and help them to grow and develop, are leaders who get the most discretionary effort from their people. These are the leaders who leave a legacy when they go in terms of the development and greater contribution of their people. It is this legacy which is their long-term impact and it is one which will continue to pay dividends well into the future.

2. There is a great deal of evidence that many organisations are starting from a low base because of the poor standard of old managerial practice. The great contributing factor to poor performance is poor management. The good news is that this is the factor that individual managers have most control over, and if they make the choice person by person to lift their leadership, then the resultant impact on performance will be great. An individual manager needs no one's permission to make the decision to be a better leader.

3. Policies and structures within the workplace should be judged and assessed on the extent to which they facilitate growth and performance. How people are managed should be determined not with control in mind but with an eye on what is most likely to facilitate their development and to improve their performance. Senior leaders intent on transformation should subject all policies and procedures to this simple test: does this help to improve individual performance and produce better organisational outcomes.

4. It is possible to make the shift from poor leadership to excellent leadership but it takes awareness and discipline. The quality of leadership in an organisation is not a given, it is something that can be changed. The world's best at some stage decided to take the lead and to invest in their leadership capability. It is something that is available to everyone, but like most things in life the shift from good to great is not easy.

5. Increasingly, we live in a world that is described as VUCA – volatile, uncertain, complex, ambiguous. This calls for new thinking about leadership as a collective act, not a positional attribute. We need leadership in, and from, our people. We need more from all – not more hours, but more ideas, more challenge,

more empathy, more care – it's a different contribution, but one that will have greater impact.

We need people in teams who are confident in their abilities, but also confident in their potential to contribute more but in a different way. Teams are the design feature of the future, but teams where it is not just participation, but personal contribution that is required.

6. Authenticity has become the major driving force in leadership today. For a workforce which is engaged and empowered, it is inspiration they seek and they find this not from distant, albeit charismatic, leaders but in leaders who believe deeply in the potential of the people they lead. The leaders who are creating the future are those who are shifting the power from the top and distributing it throughout the workplace and at the same time give people the confidence in their greater ability to lead.

The decision to build leadership capability and to develop the skills of breakthrough leadership cannot be accomplished by some group process alone. Whilst a group consensus on the need for change is a powerful force for change, the actual process itself must be decided upon and embarked upon individual by individual. This is not a process that occurs simply by osmosis although there is a key role for the impact of modelling and informal influence. It is essentially a decision, and a commitment, made by dedicated individuals who are determined to be the best leaders that they can be for the people they lead.

For those who find that the required attributes don't come easily or naturally, it starts with building mindsets that are conducive to growth and development. No one is born as a perfect leader. All managers need to make it part of their professional repertoire and like all things, when there is a commitment to excellence, it takes time and effort and focus. Experience shows that leadership can be developed to build organisations that are both good for business and good for people. Breakthrough leaders have the belief and the commitment that is crucial in achieving the vision.

The way that this leadership is displayed is grounded in one fundamental belief, and that is that we are all a work in progress, each with the capacity to grow and to develop and that it is by uncovering and removing the impediments to this development that leaders make their greatest contribution to the future. Changing mindsets, empowering people and helping them to develop to their true potential is the greatest gift that leaders give to the people that they lead and the communities that they serve.

Postscript

Management has been enshrined in organisational practice since the Industrial Revolution. It was borrowed from the military and the church, two institutions that were accustomed to managing large numbers of workers, and adopted as the best approach for managing the large number of unskilled workers who came off the land and into the newly created factories. The driving force of management was supervision, with power embedded in hierarchy, and reinforced through bureaucratic rules and processes.

This approach worked well as it was psychologically sound and self-reinforcing. You put a bunch of people addicted to control in charge of those who don't want to, or are not allowed to be responsible and you have a compelling co-dependency. Human emotion and passion were driven out by remote bosses and the application of standard operating procedures, all of which were designed to reduce uncertainty and increase predictability and whilst it produced stability, it was at the cost of performance.

Command and control became deeply embedded in the managerial psyche and highly resistant to change. The world we have today however, which is volatile, uncertain, complex, and ambiguous, calls for a new approach to managing and leading people. This has resulted in the shift in mindset from management to leadership and a shift in style from directing to empowering. We have gone from driving emotion out to building emotion in. Engagement is paramount, and collaboration and innovation are central drivers of growth. This has required us to re-imagine leadership as less a role and more a human capability.

All humans are capable of displaying leadership whether in work, in sport, in the home or in the community. The best business leaders develop this as a source of significant competitive advantage and are driven to develop greater leadership in people and teams, not take leadership away. The challenges of the new global marketplace have meant that leadership can no longer come from the few, it now must come from the many. We need more engagement, greater ownership and strong collective empowerment at the frontline if we are to survive and thrive.

The need to build and rebuild trust in our institutions, corporations and political leadership has resulted in a demand for leaders who are authentic. That is, leaders who say what they mean, and mean what they say. It is leaders driven by a deeper purpose beyond self- interest and who are genuine, rather than role playing or reading a script. The leaders who stand out are those who stand for something and those guided by a clear set of values and ethical principles. It is purpose, passion and principles that are the hallmark of leadership today and it is authenticity that is the social currency that is required.

For a workforce which is engaged and empowered, it is inspiration they seek and they find this not from charismatic or distant leaders but in leaders who believe deeply in what they do and believe deeply in the potential of the people they lead. They respect leaders who put the spotlight on the team, not on themselves, who put leadership into the teams, not take it from the teams. The leaders who are creating the future are those who are shifting the power from the executive and distributing it at all levels throughout the organization.In this way purpose and potential are redefining the practice of leadership today.

Further information and resources can be found by contacting me at www.leadership.com.au

Terry Lee
LeadershipPsychology Australia